MISTER CARNEGIE'S LIB'ARY

MISTER CARNEGIE'S LIB'ARY
CAROLINE E. WERKLEY

AMERICAN HERITAGE PRESS   NEW YORK

For My Mother
One of Mister Carnegie's Librarians

MISTER CARNEGIE'S LIB'ARY

When I was very young, I thought Andrew Carnegie lived in Moberly, Missouri (population 12,000, smack dab between St. Louis and Kansas City), because he gave Moberly what we natives called the Lib'ary. Possibly he lived in the big red brick house at the end of Fifth Street, the one with the tennis court and the curved drive, or perhaps in the yellow stone mansion with tall white pillars on West Reed Street. They were both immense solid buildings similar to the library, and certainly appropriate as a dwelling for a man of Mr. Carnegie's importance.

When I was older and wise enough to know that Mr. Carnegie would have sniffed at anything less than a sixty-six-room castle, my mother, one of Mr. Carnegie's high priestesses, and my two sisters and I went to New York. From behind a tall iron-spike fence we gazed respectfully for a long while one day at the Fifth Avenue mansion in which Mr.

Carnegie had lived, noting with pleasure the handsome pink brick, imposing enough for one of his own libraries. We half expected to see Mr. Carnegie's ghost peering out at his Moberly librarian from one of the windows of his walnut-paneled study. But no Mr. Carnegie appeared, just as there had been no Nicholas Murray Butler all summer at the Butler residence on Morningside Drive. Mother had rented rooms for herself and three daughters right across the street, sideways, from Mr. Butler's house, there being nothing available near Mr. Carnegie's. Mr. Butler was the president of Columbia University, where she was taking library courses, while Helen and Eloise went to Teachers College. I, being only thirteen, was experimented on in education classes by budding teachers.

Each of us was expected by Mother to look out the window once a day in hope that we could glimpse Mr. Butler—"just to say you've seen him"—although Helen and Eloise were much more interested in seeing a good-looking university student than Mr. Butler, and I would rather see the dogs being paraded on leashes across the street in Morningside Park.

Just as Mr. Butler was never at his windows, now there was nothing but plain glass in Mr. Carnegie's, not a ghost nor anything alive.

"I simply don't believe it," Mother said suddenly, with an alarming vehemence, and I knew exactly what she meant. We didn't believe it when we read it in a book, and we certainly didn't believe it now, looking at the fine respectability of Mr. Carnegie's house.

"Imagine Mr. Carnegie being called a robber, an octopus. I never heard anything so ridiculous. There wasn't a crooked bone in his body. That fine man, the Giver of Libraries."

And that, of course, settled the question. Mr. Carnegie was at that moment wiped clean of all evil, all capitalistic, octopusian tentacles. He was ennobled and made pure in every way, absolved forever by his Moberly librarian's faith.

Mother's—and Mr. Carnegie's—library was a square, solid gray stone building with pillars and pigeons decorating its front. The pillars Mother was proud of. I am not sure whether they were Doric or Corinthian or just plain Moberly in design, but they were stout impressive columns of stone, giving the library a proper dignity and tone. The pigeons embarrassed her. They would not stay on the roof but kept floating down to the steps or walk, and people got into the habit of looking up warily before ascending the library steps. Mother never knew what to say when people came angrily up to the desk from outdoors, saying, "Those pigeons!"

There even were board meetings about the problem, but no one knew exactly what to recommend, because pigeons were—well, you know pigeons. And a shame, too, because they were pretty birds, tame enough to eat out of your hand. They made a soft cooing sound that was pleasant, and when they were fluttering up on the roof they somehow gave a sort of literary tone to the building. But when a library patron started up the steps, it was an altogether different matter. At a board meeting, someone suggested shooting the pigeons with BB guns, but the board president, who fed birds from a window box at her home, cried out, "Murder the little wild creatures? Instill in our youth the idea of killing? Put guns in their hands, to kill, to murder?"

Another board member, who had asked enthusiastically if anyone had ever tasted pigeon pie, wished he hadn't said anything at all, and when the meeting was over no one yet knew what to do about the pigeons.

It was Mother who thought up the solution. It worked in gardens, so why wouldn't it work on a roof? She got the idea when she looked at the little white rags tied to stakes around our garden to frighten away the sparrows. Of course it would never do to have rags blowing from Mr. Carnegie's roof, tangling and tattering in the wind, frightening the pigeons, perhaps, but giving the library a ramshackle look. But a neat little plush kitty was a different story, an imitation kitty tied to a spire, turning and pouncing on the roof and frightening the pigeons away from the library. And it did work. The pigeons flew over to the top of the Fourth Street Theater across the street and settled there—but that was the theater's problem, that had nothing to do with the library.

Mr. Carnegie's Lib'ary was devoted to culture and the mind on the first floor, but its basement was given over to business. The Chamber of Commerce lived there, and at one time the Red Cross and other smaller organizations came and went. It irritated Mother that the pursuit of learning had to share the library building with the crass workings of business, and sometimes actually give way to the basement tenants when there were meetings or conventions.

"Those loud dirty men," Mother would say furiously when noise crept unwanted up the stairs to her area of authority. "They shout and smoke and spit and what-all, and never give a thought to what's above them."

The fact that they were the same men she spoke to with friendliness on the street, or sat comfortably beside in church, was of no consequence. They may have been gentlemen anyplace else, but when they invaded the library with their noise and what-all, that was a different matter.

The minute you entered the library you knew you were in some place absolutely different from anything else in Moberly. It was not only the rows and rows of books; it was the smell of paste and people, and the soft little noises that wouldn't be sounds at all except in the library, the quiet turning of magazine pages and rustling of newspapers, the cautious tread of a footstep, the surreptitious crunch of a bar of candy.

The first thing you saw in the library was Mother sitting at the half-moon-shaped golden-oak desk. She looked very imposing and majestic rising above the desk, but if you were to glance inside, you would see that she had her legs curled around the rungs of the high stool. She was perched on a pile of books stacked high on the stool, not the best new ones, of course, but some old Kathleen Norris or Grace Livingston Hill Lutz, whose literary merit she regarded as distinctly inferior.

Mother judged people by their reading habits, and she was proudest, perhaps, of Ben Jacks, who lived in the library. That is, he lived in the library as much as anyplace else, because he had no home at all. He slept nights in the railroad station, spent the mornings in the post office and his afternoons and evenings in the library. Ben Jacks limped and walked with a cane, and he ate candy while he read. Eating was forbidden in the library, but Mother pretended she did not see it. He read the best magazines and *The New York Times*, and this made up for the fact that he was disobeying a rule. Mother herself liked to eat while she read and often did so at home. It was her belief that anyone who delved so deeply in the *Times* was bound to be a superior sort of person, even if he did sleep in the railroad station. Sometimes Ben Jacks took naps in the library, leaning back comfortably in the rocking chair by the window. Unless he was holding on to *The New York Times* when he fell asleep, Mother did not disturb him.

Three other persons in Moberly besides Ben Jacks also read *The New York Times* daily, but Ben Jacks usually got it first, and I think Mother was secretly glad. She knew that the library and Mr. Carnegie meant more to Ben Jacks than to anyone else in Moberly except herself. Most people, she was sure, took the library and Mr. Carnegie's beneficence for granted, but Mr. Jacks received too much from the library to regard it with nonchalance. It was his home as well as his hobby. He and Mother had even discussed Mr. Carnegie together, and Mother said you could tell he had a fine mind; he agreed with everything she said.

Ben Jacks held a particular fascination for me. I had heard that when he was younger he had been a house mover. I had seen a house being moved only once in my life, but I had never witnessed anything as spectacular. Instead of being safely attached to a yard, where all houses belonged, this house rode slowly down the street. I have forgotten what it moved on and where it was going. It remains only a blurred and wonderful memory in my mind, a house, unlike the legendary mountain, going to Moham- med. Surely not more than two or three houses in Moberly had ever been moved from their original moorings—one of them was our own house, which had been moved long ago—so how Ben Jacks lived after and between the few jobs of his lifetime I do not know. Rumor had it that a house fell on him and that was why he was lame. I have a feeling that he was always what some people would call lazy and what Mother and I would call the cultured type. Possibly it suited him fine that people never wanted their houses moved. That gave him all the more time for attending to the world that was his reality. The unreality he endured was his bench bed in the station and his morning room at the post office.

The other two constant intellectuals in the library were the Count and Mr. Belden. Mr. Belden had a substantial hardware business and took trips around the world. A few persons in Moberly had been to Europe once in their lives, but certainly no one else had been around the world, so everyone considered him peculiar.

I think Mr. Belden loathed Ben Jacks but felt a cultural responsibility for him. He was Ben Jacks's meal ticket. He provided Ben with driblets of cash with which Ben bought his meals at the station sandwich counter. The cash also covered the noisy paper bags of candy that were Ben Jacks's daily luxury. He always selected a good magazine and a comfortable rocking chair by the window, then opened a bag of sugary lemon drops. A nap sandwiched between *The New York Times* and *Theatre Arts* rested him for an evening with the *Atlantic Monthly* and *National Geographic*. Ben Jacks actually felt superior, in spite of his limp and his shabby clothes, to most of the men in Moberly. He toiled not, neither did he spin, and yet he lived a good life. I do not think he was particularly grateful to Mr. Belden for providing him with the necessities of living. Mr. Belden had money; why should he not divide it? Mr. Jacks, with nothing in the world to share, except possibly his ideas, was by nature an actual if not professing communist, in the true sense of the word.

Mr. Belden did not toil very much either. He frequented his business only when more pressing things such as trips to Europe did not demand his attention. A long-standing and almost childish feud existed between him and Ben Jacks about *The New York Times*. They fought for it. They hovered around the desk at mail time waiting for it to be unwrapped and put in the rack along with the *Christian Science Monitor* and the *Chicago Tribune* and, of course, the *Moberly Monitor-Index*.

Also hovering and often swifter than either of them was the Count. His real name was Mr. Marchand, but Mother and I always referred to him by the title we had given him; it seemed to become him. He was a courtly gentleman who seemed much above his official position, which was secretary of the Moberly Chamber of Commerce. Someone had told us that the Count lived in a room bare of all furniture but a table and a wooden board that he slept on. Although we half believed this, because it was so weird and mysterious, we could never truly in our minds place him in any background but that of an old Southern mansion, or a French château, or a London townhouse. He was always immaculately dressed, and he called Mother "Madame," and he read strange, ancient books on spiritualism that no one else in Moberly ever asked for. If he got *The New York Times* first he read every item in it, so that it was hours before Mr. Belden or Ben Jacks could lay hands on it. Ben Jacks would limp restlessly about the periodical room, stopping frequently to stare rudely over the Count's shoulder, and Mr. Belden would come up to the desk at least two or three times to complain bitterly and loudly about people who hogged the newspapers.

Mother was extremely fond of most of her library patrons, but she had a keen dislike for one of them, Mr. Medley. True, he was a *New York Times* reader, but he had done an unforgivable thing. He had shown Mother an article in a book that referred to Mr. Carnegie as a financial octopus, a pirate, a violent and ruthless grabber for power.

"Strange old chap, wasn't he?" Mr. Medley said as he looked up sneeringly at Mr. Carnegie's grim, aristocratic portrait, which dominated the library entrance. "What was the cost of his little old libraries to him, with all those millions he fleeced the public out of? Not a drop in the bucket, no sir, not even a little drop in a great big bucket."

Mother did not put Mr. Medley's book back on the shelves. She sat on it instead, along with Grace Livingston Hill Lutz.

Mother was so much a part of the library that it

never occurred to me—or, I am sure, to her—that anything, certainly not Miss Pearl Horner, could disrupt our way of life and threaten her position as Mr. Carnegie's most admiring employee. The threat, the undreamed-of danger, came on a board meeting night. For this important occasion Mother always wore a silk dress and her little round gold watch fastened to a fleur-de-lis, and she got a marcel. The Private Room—really the office—which we both regarded as very special and ours alone, was dusted and swept and the piles of books were arranged neatly, for it was in this room that the board held their meetings. How we hated sharing the Private Room with anyone else! Here all the new books were unpacked, and we greedily took our pick of them before they went on the shelves. Here, while waiting to walk home with Mother, I frequently curled up in one of the big black leather chairs with a *National Geographic* or Sara Teasdale's poems and, like Ben Jacks, munched on lemon drops. Or lay lazily on the black leather couch and admired the elegant, greenish-colored fireplace at one end of the room. The carved mantle was top-heavy with marble statues, stuffed birds under a glass dome, and other *objets d'art* that people had donated with embarrassment to the library, things too bizarre or too ancient for their own homes but too valuable to discard.

When I saw the board members leave the library after this particular meeting, I made a loud cracking noise with a pile of magazines so that Ben Jacks would realize it was closing time. For a moment I clasped *Theatre Arts* close to my breast and imagined I was Katherine Cornell making an entrance onto the stage. How the audience clapped, how the lights shone! Then, regretfully, I left the stage and went into the office. Mother was sitting very still in front of the golden-oak roll-top desk, and I knew immediately that something was wrong. Usually she was in high spirits after a board meeting.

"What's the matter, are you sick?" I asked anxiously.

"You know Pearl Horner," Mother said.

"Of course I do." Pearl Horner had worked in the library last summer, a large blonde girl who went back to college in the fall.

"Pearl wants to be librarian," Mother said lifelessly.

"But *you're* librarian!"

"Pearl has a degree in Library Science now. She told the board about the new methods she learned. It made a big impression on Mr. Albans and some of the others. Not that she could improve anything here. I read the library journals, I go to the conventions. Of course," Mother mused, "they aren't planning on a thing yet. It's just that they mentioned it to me, and I know some of them think Pearl might be a better librarian because of her degree."

"But you went to college," I argued. I was always

fascinated by the college Mother had gone to. Her school days had been so long ago that the college no longer existed, but it had had a wonderful name, Central Female Academy.

"They didn't have Library Science then," Mother explained. "Not at Central, anyway." She had taken German and painting and philosophy, and our house was filled with hand-painted china, German grammars, and philosophy books. But she had not learned to be a librarian in college. That had come when she worked as an assistant in the library after my father died. She had pasted torn pages and book jackets, catalogued books, stacked magazines, kept files, checked books in and out, pored over book lists, placated board members, and done all the countless things that must be taken care of in a library. Only on Saturday nights after work did she find time to do what people thought librarians spent all their time doing—read books. And now here was Miss Pearl Horner, a snip of a girl armed with determination and a degree, trying to persuade the library board that they needed a librarian with more education.

"What will we do?" I whispered. And, after a moment's thought, "What will happen to Ben Jacks?"

It was *The New York Times*, of course, that saved the library for us. Mother's library files had innumerable clippings from the *Times* about Columbia University in New York. And now everything seemed amazingly clear. Helen and Eloise, who had just started teaching careers, wanted to go to summer school, and Mother would go, too, and study Library Science. We would all go—to Columbia University, holy of holies as far as library schools were concerned. *That* would fix Pearl Horner, who certainly had never studied at such a sacred place.

In those days the university offered true hospitality to its summer students. "Columbia is going to *meet* us," Mother told us excitedly. I would not have been surprised if the representative chosen to welcome us had been Mr. Butler himself, but we were all perfectly satisfied to be rescued from Grand Central Station by a nice young student wearing a red carnation in his buttonhole for identification.

At that period life was surely not so hectic, and universities were not so demanding, because there always seemed to be time left over from studying to explore New York and to watch for artists and writers and other well-known persons. Mother said if we saw a famous man to go right up to him and tell him our names—he would be flattered that people all the way from Missouri knew who he was.

Before the summer was over, as a special treat, Mother and I went for a hansom-cab ride in Central Park. We listened eagerly to what our driver said and craned our necks to see landmarks that he pointed out. He was familiar not only with everything in the park but with almost all that could be seen from it. At one point he waved his hand vaguely toward Fifth Avenue and rattled off a list of houses that were then or were at one time owned by famous rich men. Among them was Mr. Carnegie's. Mother and I looked at each other smugly. Of course we knew all about Mr. Carnegie's house, probably much more than our hansom-cab driver. Did he know there was a pipe organ near the grand staircase, and that the house had two main boilers of a type and size used in ocean-going liners? That a mining car transported coal from the bunker to the stoking floor, running on its own track and turntable? And that the house had five elevators, including one small one with a black leather seat used exclusively by Mr. Carnegie's widow? We were only from Missouri, but there weren't any flies on us when it came to information about Mr. Carnegie. The house, we could have told him, cost one million dollars when it was built in 1900.

"Them old robbers," our driver suddenly said vehemently, giving his horse a slash with his whip as though the poor animal was somehow responsible for his anger.

"What old robbers?" Mother asked, bewildered, wondering at the strange way the travelogue had digressed.

"Vanderbilt, Morgan, Carnegie, all them rich thieves, bloodsuckers, they took the bread right out of the poor man's mouth and never said so much as 'thank you.'"

Mother's voice was cold and terrible sounding. "Did you refer to Mr. Carnegie?" she asked, and I knew something dreadful was going to happen. "Mr. *Andrew* Carnegie?"

"Old Carnegie himself. Biggest crook these United States has seen. Steel, iron, railroads, nothin' he wouldn't put his hands on. His house there is built on bodies, lady, on bodies of the poor."

"Stop your horse!" Mother shouted, and the driver, alarmed, drew his gentle horse to a stop and turned around to stare at Mother.

"How dare you say such things about Mr. Carnegie?" Mother cried out angrily. "Do you know that I am an employee of Mr. Carnegie's?"

The driver looked at her in amazement. "Of that old duff's?" he asked incredulously. "He's dead and gone, that old robber is, nobody works for him."

"Mr. Carnegie will *never* die," Mother said, not angrily now, but firmly, her eyes glowing. "Mr. Carnegie will live forever in his libraries, and I"— she repeated this proudly—"*I* am one of his librarians."

With this exit line Mother and I got out of the hansom cab. Mother paid the cab driver half of his fare, since our drive was only halfway completed, and imperiously waved him on. We lost our way in the park and wandered around for hours before we knew where we were, but we did not blame each other. "Just keep the general direction of Mr. Carnegie's house in mind," Mother kept saying, "and we'll come out all right."

When we returned to Moberly at the end of summer the plush kitty was still dangling on top of the library roof, but the pigeons had all come back from the Fourth Street Theater. They knew by then that the kitty was only make-believe and would not spring at them. "Library pigeons," Mother said, "would naturally be intelligent pigeons."

But we knew something was wrong when we did not see Ben Jacks in the library the first day we were there. Ben Jacks had gone crazy, Mr. Medley told us rather triumphantly. He had taken to jumping out at women on dark corners, holding a newspaper over his head to try to hide his face. He had used old issues of *The New York Times*, stolen from the library. Mr. Belden did not ask for the *Times* at all any more. Mostly he just sat in Ben Jacks's chair and stared in front of him, shaking his head.

We were something of a mild sensation for a while, a complete family educated at Columbia University, from a fifty-three-year-old mother down to a thirteen-year-old daughter, with two daughters, aged nineteen and twenty, in between. Mother always took great care to explain that we had been to Columbia University in New York, so it would not be confused with the state university at Columbia, Missouri, where *any*body could go.

Oh, yes, we had brushed elbows with writers and artists and had seen where great and important people lived, including Mr. Andrew Carnegie. Mother gave talks on this at high-school assembly, at Thursday Club, at the Daughters of Susanna Wesley Missionary Society, and, of course, to the library board. Soon afterward she got a raise in salary. She now made sixty-five dollars a month. The day the library board notified her of this salary increase I noticed her looking benevolently at the portrait of Mr. Carnegie. I am sure she was thanking him for the raise. Then she looked sadly over in the corner by the steps where Ben Jacks's battered old hat and frayed coat always used to hang, and I know that she felt something important was gone from the library. I think Mr. Carnegie felt this, too. His picture was looking darker and grimmer and lonelier than ever. . . .

2

THE CHAPERONE

A few of the male patrons of Mr. Carnegie's Lib'ary probably lost some of their interest in books and library browsing during the summer I served as chaperone to the librarian. They doubtless found it unsettling to be followed about from stack to stack by an owl-eyed child who took her duties very seriously, pressing closely and protectively against the librarian when any of the gentlemen approached her for book information, or staring at them balefully if they simply commented courteously to her on the weather or the affairs of the nation.

I was about eight years of age when I started my library career as chaperone to my mother, and, while keeping an eye on her, I also wielded the rubber date stamp with a flourish as I sat in splendor behind the charging desk. If any of my friends happened to be in the library when I was presiding, this was an added glory. I stamped a little harder

and more officiously for them to show my importance. They might be prettier or more popular on
the school grounds, but when they were in my
castle they had better watch their step. *My* mother
was the queen of the castle, and therefore I was the
princess.

Naturally Mother had too much regard for the
dignity of her office and the possible disapproval of
the library board to allow me to serve at the circulation desk often. I came in very handy, however, for
other minor chores, such as straightening up the
periodical room at closing time, and escorting
visiting dogs and cats from the library — mainly our
own little dog, Laddie, who found it difficult to
understand why, if one of us was in the library, he
should not be there also. If Laddie would only lie
quietly under the circulation desk so no one would
know he was there, or even hide safely in the
Private Room, he could come in the library, Mother
told us when we complained about Laddie's exclu-
sion from our second home. But there was no telling
when he would take a dislike to a particular library
patron and dart out from behind the circulation
desk and bite him, thus jeopardizing not only his
own life — a mad dog could be shot — but Mother's
position, and thus the very bread in our mouths.
And it made people furious to be suddenly snarled
at and threatened when they were peacefully book
browsing back in the stacks. For some reason,
Laddie seemed to think it was *he* who was Mother's

library chaperone.

It was understood, though, by both Mother and myself, that the chaperoning was my job. The reason I was appointed to this unpaid but important post was because a middle-aged man, who had rented an apartment in our house, was a library browser.

In our home, as long as I can remember, there were always two rooms that did not belong to us. The house was ours, mortgage free; Mother had bought it after my father's death when she returned with her little girls to the town where she had been born and had grown up, and where her mother still lived. But the apartment that was rented never really seemed to be part of our house. I caught glimpses of the inside of it sometimes when I passed by and a door was open. Sometimes I was even invited in, and then I saw it all, but it still retained its strangeness. It belonged to a succession of tenants, mostly young couples or respectable women. It was the Apartment Upstairs, a place inhabited by outsiders, removed from the rest of our home as completely as though it were still sitting, by some miracle, in the middle of the empty lot on the corner, where once our house had stood.

The renter was the intruder, the stranger in our house, but we knew him well and respected him, because his financial contribution augmented Mother's salary as librarian. He was the Extra Money Needed, the Coal Bill Paid, the New Winter Coat, Laddie's Dog Tax. We saw him walking down

Logan Street, a For Rent section of the paper in his hand, and we nodded knowingly to each other and waited. He was Helen's Trombone Lessons approaching, hesitating and unaware, peering and squinting at the house addresses, making a false stop or two before finally reaching No. 406. The renter had arrived. And the Apartment Upstairs was waiting for him.

My sisters and I did not like the intrusion of renters in our home, and neither did Laddie. They did not have the smell of permanency, of belonging, of proper family to him, and they had better watch their p's and q's when he was around. Mother did not like sharing her house with strangers, either, but if her daughters were to have the advantages she wished to give them, advantages which she herself had been given, and which girls should have if they were to enjoy and contribute to the cultural heritage of their country, she must somehow secure more income than that of her salary as librarian and the dividends earned by the small capital left her by my father.

Mr. Carnegie's own mother had not been too proud to use a room of her house as a little vegetable and sweet shop in order to keep her sons in school. It was equally true that by the time Andrew Carnegie was Helen's age he was out delivering telegrams and bringing his salary home to his mother. But Mr. Carnegie, even as a child, had been an aggressive, ambitious person. Mother had read his autobiography, as well as a flattering biography of him written by a long-time admirer, and innumerable magazine articles concerning him. (Of course she discounted anything she read about him that was unfavorable — such articles were motivated by envy.) Her own daughters, she had to admit, seemed to lack the proper get-up-and-go necessary to forge ahead in the world, and thus had to be provided with good educations that would automatically provide them with proper backgrounds in preparation for respectable professions.

When any of Mother's friends suggested sensibly that Helen and Eloise, who were in their teens, be allowed to earn a little money in the summertime by working in Woolworth's, Mother was as outraged as Mr. Carnegie's mother was when one of her friends suggested that her young son Andrew might peddle knickknacks around the wharves. Mother was fond of telling us Mrs. Carnegie's reaction to this suggestion, which Mr. Carnegie had told about in his autobiography.

"I would rather throw him into the Allegheny River," Mrs. Carnegie had cried.

We never doubted that Mother, as fierce as Mrs. Carnegie, would throw us in the quarry or Forest Park lake rather than expose us to a wrong environment. Somehow Mother felt that no profession was as proper and respectable for us as schoolteaching, and it was for this that we had to bide our time, acquiring a cultural background while she worked and we waited.

Eloise and Helen and I finally began to understand the importance and necessity of outsiders invading our home the year that Helen developed a passionate yearning to take trombone lessons. Mother, to whom music was a high form of culture—we were expected to listen to Galli-Curci's and Caruso's records, even though we insisted also on "The Sheik of Araby" and "Yes! We Have No Bananas"—was proud of, although slightly bewildered by, her oldest daughter's ambition to be a trombonist. It would be nice if any of us could sing like Galli-Curci, but a trombonist was better than nothing.

One day, when a middle-aged man knocked at the door, Helen peered through the living-room window that looked out onto the front porch.

"A renter," she sniffed. "A funny-looking old renter with whiskers."

"Where's Mother?" Eloise asked. "I don't want to show the apartment to a funny-looking old man."

"She's next door at the Nevinses'," Helen answered, pulling aside the window curtain in order to inspect the hopeful renter a little better. "I'm not going to show it, either. Everybody would laugh if they saw a funny-looking old man like that going in and out of our house."

"I'm not going to show the apartment to Old Funny Whiskers, either," I stated firmly, proud of asserting myself. So the three of us stood at the window, staring out at the bewildered man who had sought and found 406 West Logan, only to discover that it did not want him.

As he walked off the porch Mother came running into the house from the back door. "Where is he?" she asked breathlessly. "Mrs. Nevins said a renter was over here, she saw him come up on the porch."

All of us looked guilty. Finally Helen blurted out, "An old funny face like that. Why do we have to rent our apartment to *him*? Why do we have to rent our apartment at all, anyway? Why can't we be like other people and let the house just be ours?"

Mother thought hopelessly of the rows of figures in her account book which proved that income barely kept up with outgo. She thought of her library salary of sixty dollars a month, of Eloise wanting to go to Girl Reserve camp, and Helen wanting to take trombone lessons, and of the fifty cents she paid each week to my elocution teacher. She stared out of the window despairingly at the retreating figure of a man with money in his pocket for an apartment.

"An old funny face," she said, "but he had the money for your trombone lessons in his pocket, Helen."

Suddenly we understood. Everything seemed to come clear to us. The prospective renter was not a whiskered intruder walking off down the street. He was a Girl Reserve summer camp, with tennis courts and a lake for swimming . . . he was a bag full of cherry and lemon suckers from old Mr. Barnes's

Confectionary . . . he was a golden horn, shiny and brass and long desired, uttering rapturous low moans of song.

Helen stared at Mother in misery, moaned as sadly and piteously as her own trombone, and then ran out the door after Old Funny Whiskers. We watched her catch up with him, stop him, and talk frantically, smiling and pointing toward our house. Then we saw him turn around, rather dazed, and walk back with her. Mother ran out to meet him as though he were an old friend.

Among ourselves we always called him the Gentleman, not Funny Whiskers at all. Maybe it was because of the big words he used and the strange books he read from the high back shelves at the library. At first Mother worried at having rented our apartment to a single man — even though he had character references — because people might talk.

"The three girls and Mama are right here with me every minute I'm home, but you know neighbors," Mother said darkly. Mother was no innocent. It was well-known that one flashy-looking woman in town, a widow like Mother, and the owner of a big brick house, rented her rooms to gentlemen only, fly-by-night salesmen who were probably, sniffed Mother, up to no good.

"No gentleman," Mother said meaningfully to Grandmother, "is in one night, out the next morning, not even giving his right name, most likely."

Mother was a great believer in appearances. As a widow and the mother of three daughters, she felt she must be very careful of her reputation, especially since she was out in the working world where men were sometimes inclined to be coarse in ways they would never dare to be in their homes. Not that any man had ever been coarse to *her*—possibly because male library patrons really had their minds on books. Nevertheless, one did not take chances.

But now here a gentleman was at 406 West Logan, accepted hastily and gratefully in a time of financial stress, and we had to make the best of it. Mother never doubted that he *was* a gentleman, however, because he owned so many books, even a set of Shakespeare. These were the best recommendations he could have. In the daytime the Gentleman worked at the Wabash shops, but at night and on weekends he read. He spent a great deal of his free time with his own library, which he had brought in several cardboard cartons and had piled on all of the tables, in the cupboard, on top of the icebox, and on window sills, even stacking many books on the floor. Still, he often came to the library at night and wandered around in the back section, poking at the books in philosophy and theology that most people in Moberly passed over. On these nights Mother would call home and whisper, "One of you girls come down and walk home with me tonight. It's just best," she would say warily. Since my older sisters were almost always busy with dates and grown-up activities, it was usually I who ran down to watch over Mother. I was, after all, no novice at chaperoning. My sisters had utilized me for this purpose when I was even younger, during a period when Mother had been briefly courted by an admirer from her girlhood who was now a widower.

"Stay with her all the time," Eloise had whispered to me when the widower came to call on Mother. "Don't leave them alone for a minute. And if he stays very long, tell Mother you don't feel good, you think you're getting the mumps." She and Helen were too sophisticated to be rude in front of grown-ups, but a young child could show she did not like an interloper in the household and get away with it. None of us truly disliked Mother's old friend—he brought us boxes of candy and tickets to the picture show—it was just that we did not want him for our father.

Actually the Gentleman was never so ungentlemanly as to suggest walking home with Mother from the library, and it was because I had so little chaperoning to do as far as he was concerned that I extended my watch to any other men who looked at all suspicious to me, even to the extent of appearing suddenly and frighteningly among the stacks like Laddie, and scowling at a male patron if he spoke to Mother, or came too close to her. On the few occasions when Laddie and I made a sudden appearance together in the stacks, I frowning, and Laddie snarling, book lovers usually decided they had had enough of the library, free books or no free books.

The Gentleman himself kept well out of Mother's way, understanding, after a day or so, that he had made a dreadful mistake in his choice of a home. He possibly had no objections to financing trombone lessons, but listening to them was too much. Helen was thorough in her practice. Up, down, up, down, would go the beautiful golden slide, producing haunted, guttural tones. Mother, for the sake of culture, adjusted herself. Laddie, whose ears were sensitive, usually ran away for a few hours, or, if he were trapped indoors, bayed mournfully while Helen blew. Eloise and I, for reasons of family connections, endured. Also, we knew that Helen had to listen to our cultural probings—Eloise on the piano, and I with elocution lessons. The Gentleman, who had neither cultural nor family reasons to help him, agonized.

One Sunday afternoon, when Helen was practicing, I passed by the Gentleman's open door. He was sitting before the French windows with a book in his hand, but he was not looking at it. He was muttering something over and over, staring fixedly before him, and I wondered if he took elocution lessons, too. I moved into the room, although we were forbidden by Mother to enter the renter's apartment except by invitation.

"Beauty is truth, truth beauty," the Gentleman was saying.

"What's that?" I asked him, my manners completely forgotten.

From below came a loud, harsh bellow of sound, and the Gentleman winced.

"It's a sort of medicine," he said, "saturation of the mind. My old friend John Keats is the doctor."

"Dr. Keats," I said reflectively. "I don't know him, only Dr. Merry, our Cousin Jesse."

But the Gentleman was paying no attention to me.

"Thou still unravished bride of quietness,
Thou foster-child of silence and slow time . . ."

He was not talking to me at all, but out of the window at nothing, so, knowing my unimportance, I walked from his room and into the unpuzzling din of Helen's horn.

Helen reached the peak of culture and attainment soon thereafter when she learned to play "Smilin' Through."

"And two eyes of blue" . . . umph, umph, umph, umph, umph . . . "come smilin' through," . . . umph, umph, umph, umph, "at me."

We all knew "Smilin' Through," each beat, each staccato, each fortissimo, each measured chord. Helen played slowly and carefully, every note conquered, her rendition exactly as the piece demanded, no flighty improvisations, but all chords consisting of the correct C, G, and E.

"Better to go slow," Mother said approvingly, "than to fly through it and miss some of the notes."

To miss some of the notes would be to waste money. The piece was printed as it was supposed to be. One paid for it as it was, and one paid to be taught to play it as it was written. Helen's slow, methodical correctness showed her appreciation not only of music and culture, but of law and order and of things as they are supposed to be.

"It would be nice," Mother said to Helen, "if someone could enjoy your performance. It's a shame to play and play and no one to hear what you can do"—forgetting the Gentleman who heard too well, and the Nevinses next door, and the Watkinses and Conrads across the street, to whom sound was wafted by the relentless, neighborly wind. "Maybe on Sunday afternoon I'll ask Cousin Ivy to drop by. And Leatha and Frank."

Helen lived "Smilin' Through" all week, and we lived it with her, Eloise even picking it out by ear on the piano so that she could accompany Helen, using a thumping, heavily accented base. I practiced a new reading given me by my elocution teacher, in case I should be called upon to perform, too. Mother made fancy sandwiches and coconut snowcreams for Sunday afternoon, and Helen tooted frantically all Sunday morning, for one last practice.

Cousin Ivy and Cousins Leatha and Frank ate the sandwiches and coconut snowcreams and settled back to hear the trombone selection, knowing that this was important to Mother, their Cousin Carrie, that it was something that must be done, and that one afternoon, after all, was not an eternity.

The golden horn gleamed in the Sunday sun. Helen gave a couple of tentative toots to get the key, and at last "Smilin' Through" was under way. She played it once, verse and chorus, and Mother signaled to her to go through it again. In the middle of the second performance we heard the Gentleman's steps coming down the stairs. But he did not go out of the front door. Instead, he paused before the door of the living room where Helen was playing, and shouted in a terrible voice, "Beauty is truth, truth beauty!"

Helen's lips left the mouthpiece and dropped open in amazement.

His shouting had not been hard to hear even above the trombone, but now in the silence his voice boomed and bellowed and he seemed unaware of it.

"O Attic shape! Fair attitude! with brede
Of marble men and maidens overwrought,
With forest branches and the trodden weed;
Thou, silent form, dost tease us out of thought
As doth eternity: Cold Pastoral!"

Mother and Helen and Eloise and I stared at the Gentleman in horror, his shouting and his strange words terrorizing us. Mother drew back and picked up one of her big hand-painted china vases. I knew she thought the Gentleman had gone crazy, and if he stepped into the room she would throw her valuable vase at him, treasure or no treasure. I had tied a red ribbon around Laddie's muzzle so that he could not howl during Helen's concert, but this did not stop him from leaping up from behind a chair, growling furiously, and tearing angrily and unsuccessfully at the ribbon with his paw so that he could perform his duty as protector properly. This attack on his family from a stranger was only what might be expected when an outsider was allowed to live in one's house. He could have told us that.

Cousin Ivy and Cousins Leatha and Frank were too startled to be afraid. This was probably the usual thing on Sunday afternoon at Cousin Carrie's. Carrie was the odd, unpredictable relative. She painted china and went around poking tacky old furniture and glassware, that she called antique and valuable, out of people's basements and attics, and she belonged to a Shakespeare Club. Anything might happen at her house.

But the Gentleman suddenly sensed our horror. He shook his head confusedly, realizing, I think for the first time, that he had been shouting and had frightened us. Then, in a quiet voice, he spoke again, as though he were merely finishing a sentence that he had begun.

"Heard melodies are sweet, but those unheard

Are sweeter . . . . John Keats, Mrs. Elsea and daughters, my friend John Keats."

As he disappeared up the stairs, Mother put the hand-painted vase down on the table and stared at it sadly. The Gentleman must go. The nice quiet Gentleman who paid his rent so regularly was a madman, even if he was a book lover, and of course must go. Helen started to play "Smilin' Through" again, but after two or three puffs which got her up the little brown road winding over the hill, she put the trombone away, into its neat black case with the orange satin lining. Suddenly she seemed to be tired of playing the trombone.

"John Keats is a doctor," I announced to Mother, feeling very important in knowing who he was, although I had no idea what the Gentleman was talking about. I untied the red ribbon from Laddie's muzzle and stuffed his mouth with snowcreams and pimento cheese sandwiches, so that he would quit snarling and trembling with fury.

But Mother was paying no attention to me. She was distractedly passing the coconut snowcreams and practicing mentally what she would say to the Gentleman to tell him he had to move.

"Shouting before the children . . . we're not used to that sort of thing, Mr. Herschel. We live quietly, and I never allow the children to shout and be noisy, and I can't have it in anyone else in the house."

We usually dreaded hearing that a renter was going to move. It was an insult to Mother if a renter wanted to leave our house. She always insisted on knowing exactly why he wanted to move, what was wrong, and where he thought he could find things as nice anywhere else as at our house, what privileges, what low rent, what heating facilities. But there was none of this with the Gentleman. He was out of his head, Mother was sure of this, and she did not want to arouse his anger, so she spoke to him gently, and he, glad of an excuse to leave the trombone-haunted Elsea house, gently agreed. He was polite and absolutely understanding. He had enjoyed our Christian home, but perhaps he would stay at the hotel, it was closer to his work. The Gentleman had also probably noticed nervously that since his outburst we did not dare unchain Laddie when he was home. Laddie began barking the moment the Enemy appeared at the end of the block, and we had to keep him supplied with extra soup bones and other delicacies so that he would not moan and carry on all the while the Gentleman was upstairs.

Helen was practicing on her trombone the day the Gentleman moved away, but she stopped her playing and, with the rest of us, even Laddie with the red ribbon on his muzzle, went to the door to see him off.

"A beautiful piece of metal," the Gentleman said thoughtfully, as he said good-by to Helen. And then, to Mother, softly, "Did you know that the playing of a wind instrument, especially by women, often causes malformation of the mouth?"

Mother stared after him as he went down Logan Street with his suitcase—his books had already preceded him in a van — and then she looked at Helen's perfect, rosebud-shaped mouth.

"What's an 'Attic shape' — or a 'silent form'?" I asked, suddenly remembering some of the words that the Gentleman had shouted to us the other day.

"It's probably a dress form," said Eloise, who was learning to sew. "Some sort of an old form that you've had up in your attic."

Mother was not listening to either of us. She was thinking of the ad she would be putting in the newspaper about our apartment. And of another ad in the "Music Instruments for Sale" section: "Trombone, good as new." And wondering if she was just imagining things, or if Helen's lips really did seem to have a slight malformation, a betrayal by Culture.

After he moved from our home, the Gentleman must have decided to spend more time with his own books, because he seldom visited the library. Although I was now no longer needed as a chaperone, I was still allowed to preside briefly and proudly at the charge desk. Mr. Carnegie, who at an early age ran shop errands for his parents, and even had the accounts of the shop customers entrusted to him, would have approved of my being asked to help out in this fashion.

Perhaps my introductory work in librarianship was not done with the speed and efficiency that is the keynote of modern automated libraries, but nevertheless the charging was performed with the authority and assurance of a princess whose mother was queen of the castle. And certainly no ogre nor dragon — nor mortal man — attacked her as long as I was her chaperone.

Laddie, of course, kept slipping into the library. He never could understand that *he* was not the library chaperone.

3
THE WONDERFUL CLIPPING COLLECTION

Little Mrs. O'Malley, for several of the months that she lived in our apartment, was the pride of Mother's life, because she had been transformed from an almost total nonreader—one naturally did not count movie magazines—into a confirmed library user. And all because of her interest in the library's wonderful clipping collection. It simply showed, as Mother told the library board triumphantly, that there were ways and means of reaching everyone in the community if a librarian used a little ingenuity and tried to understand her public.

Over the years Mother had lovingly amassed thousands of bits of news—concerning everything from aardvark to zymurgy—from magazines and newspapers and pamphlets. She valued them so highly that she had instructed the caretaker of the library that should fire occur, his first thought was to be for the shelves and cases of clippings. Books, hopefully, could be replaced. The clippings could not.

It was simply chance wandering that had brought Mrs. O'Malley to the files of the clipping department, but they took her interest immediately and completely. Her reports of the excellent clipping collection had even brought into the library other confirmed nonreaders, such as Mr. Leber and Mr. Miller. Not everyone could read and enjoy the better literature; Mother was a realist about that. If Mr. Leber wanted to read only articles about automobiles, and Mr. Miller seemed to be interested in nothing but fishing, well, the library had to be able to satisfy the curiosity of *all* of its clients. Mrs. O'Malley said eagerly that she was interested in *everything*, a remark that made Mother feel there was more intelligence in the brain beneath that pretty red hair than most people would think.

There wasn't any Mr. O'Malley. "She says he went off and left her," I heard Mother telling a neighbor indignantly. "One night he just didn't come home, and that poor little thing has had to get out and make a living as best she could."

I could not imagine Mr. O'Malley not wanting to come back to Mrs. O'Malley. She was so soft, so pretty, that I wanted to pat her as I would a kitty. She was a clerk at Bousman's Department Store, and she was just as sweet down there as she was at home.

She worked in piece goods, and whenever Mother went to Bousman's to look at material Mrs. O'Malley did not mind how many bolts of cloth she had to take out. She would unroll the exotic silks and georgettes and hold them over her hand and tell Mother to feel, wasn't it the softest, loveliest stuff she ever saw? Mother always felt the silks and georgettes and velvets, although mostly she bought the cotton. Mrs. O'Malley had a way of displaying even a simple flower-sprigged cotton, however, as though it were purple velvet, and she would hold it up against her and say, "Won't it make a perfectly lovely dress?"

One day, when Mother had wandered off to another part of the store, Mrs. O'Malley draped a beautiful bright blue piece of silk about me, and I heard her ask Mr. Miller, the floorwalker, in her soft, purry voice, "Isn't she a little darling?"

I thought I would die with pleasure and with bashfulness, but when I looked up Mr. Miller wasn't even looking at me.

"She sure is a little darling, all right," he said, but he was staring at Mrs. O'Malley, and after looking around him to see that no one but me was about, he reached out and pinched Mrs. O'Malley's white arm.

I looked at him in amazement. Why, Mrs. O'Malley hadn't done a thing to him, and he had pinched her; you could see little red marks forming a circle above her elbow. If I were Mrs. O'Malley and he had pinched me when I hadn't done a single thing to him, I would have pinched him back, or bitten him, or kicked him in the shins. Or bent one of his fingers back until he hollered "uncle."

But Mrs. O'Malley didn't do any of those things. She just smiled sweetly, and took the blue silk away from me and let a piece of it fall down in front of her, until all you could see were her shoes and her head. She twisted it about her tightly, and I thought Mr. Miller was going to pinch her again, the way he held out his hand, but Mrs. O'Malley let the silk fall all of a sudden and began to do it up in the bolt and said to me, "Where do you suppose your mother could be?" Then we went off to the glove counter to find Mother.

"Why do you suppose men are so mean to her?" I asked Eloise that evening. "She's so pretty and so little and men are so mean to her. The horrible old things."

I wished now I'd kicked Mr. Miller or bitten his hand when he pinched Mrs. O'Malley. That would have taught him a thing or two.

"Mr. O'Malley went away and she doesn't know where he is, and then Mr. Miller pinched her," I went on, puzzled.

"You mean he honest *meant* to pinch her? Just being mean?" Eloise was incredulous.

"Just being mean. I saw him. And Mrs. O'Malley was so nice, she didn't pinch back or anything. She just let him do it."

"Like in the Bible, I guess," Eloise said. "Turning your other cheek when someone hits you in the face."

"That's how it was," I marveled. "Imagine being so good you don't care if anyone hurts you."

The only thing I didn't like about Mrs. O'Malley living at our house was having to empty her ice pan. In winter the renters usually placed their butter and milk at one of the window sills, but in summer the ice was always coming in and going out again into the waiting pan under the icebox, and the pan was forever overflowing. It was my job, since Mrs. O'Malley was away all day, to go up to her kitchenette early in the afternoon and empty the water before the pan got too full to handle without spilling. One event that made up for doing this unpleasant chore was the arrival of the iceman every morning, because that meant an ice party, sitting out on the warm cement walk and crunching pieces of ice begged or snatched from the big white ice wagon. Ice cubes are all very well in their place, but they are nothing to have a party with, like the huge chunks of ice, bigger than one's fist, that we bit into, not minding the cold water dripping down our arms and all over our clothes. If it was too big to bite, it could be broken easily by a brick, or placed on the cement walk to melt into a more manageable portion.

"Hey, iceman, can I have a piece of ice?" we would shout, lunging toward the ice wagon, and if he did give us some we would carry it away in freezing hands as though it were a million dollars. If he were a new man on the job and refused us, knowing no better, we would wait until he went into the house with a square of ice fastened to his tongs, the ice dripping as he walked, and then we would swarm over the back of his wagon, reaching into the dark, burlap-covered wagon floor for stray ice splinters. Sometimes the horse would start to trot down the street, and when it did we would scream with excitement and jump off the wagon.

Nobody liked Whitey, a new iceman who took over the ice route the summer that Mrs. O'Malley lived in our house. Whitey would never let anyone have pieces of ice, even though we could see all sorts of little broken-up chunks inside the wagon.

"You kids keep offa that wagon," Whitey would growl when he started into a house with a dime's worth of ice. "If I see anyone up there in my wagon when I come back here, I'll knock their ears in."

And nobody dared get on the wagon, Whitey was so fierce. But what good was summer if you couldn't have an ice party in the morning? We could go in our houses and chip off a piece of ice to suck on, but that was not the same as getting it off the wagon, with little pieces of wood or dirt clinging to it, or tags from the burlap that covered the ice.

Mrs. O'Malley had a two weeks' vacation from Bousman's Store in August and I didn't have to empty her ice pan, so I had a vacation, too. It was sometime during those two weeks that Jack Nevins noticed the iceman was gone for ages and ages when he went in our house to deliver Mrs. O'Malley's ice.

"I bet I'd have time to climb up on the back of the wagon and get us a lot of ice and be off it before he ever got back," Jack bragged.

"Bet he dripped his old ice all over her carpet and she made him clean it up," someone snickered.

"I hope she did," Eloise said. "I hope she made him get down on his hands and knees and mop up every little spot. That old Whitey."

"Dare you to get on the wagon and get off before Whitey comes out."

"I ain't afraid." And Jack scrambled up on the wagon, while we watched anxiously for Whitey to come out and see Jack and knock his ears in.

But Jack was off the wagon and we had our ice and had hurried around to the back yard with it by the time Whitey came out, swinging his ice tongs and humming – not looking mad as though Mrs. O'Malley had made him mop up ice water on her carpet. But we didn't care what she'd made him do; we had our ice party, and Whitey never knew we'd been on the wagon.

Every morning while Mrs. O'Malley was home during her vacation we had plenty of time to get ice, and one day we grew so bold that we even sat down right on the front walk and cracked the ice and ate it, instead of running around to the back to be gone before Whitey came out. We had enough time to do all that and could have gotten more ice if we'd wanted it, Whitey was so slow coming out of the house.

"You suppose he gets her carpet dirty every morning, the reason he stays so long?" I asked Eloise one day.

"I guess he must," Eloise said, crunching her ice. "Let's go upstairs tomorrow and watch him do it, pretend we've come up to go to the bathroom and go real slow by her door so we can see him cleaning up her carpet."

Since the one bathroom in the house was upstairs, this was not an illogical project. I giggled. It was a wonderful idea. It would be fun to see mean old Whitey, his face furious and red with anger, mopping up a floor.

So the next day when Whitey went upstairs with his ice, and Jack had scrambled up on the wagon to salvage some leftover chunks, Eloise and I went softly up the stairs.

"Pretend it's you who's got to go," Eloise whispered.

"I won't do it, you pretend."

"Silly, it doesn't matter who pretends, no one will know. We'll just peek in her room as we run past, a peek will be long enough to see if he's mopping up her floor, or what he's doing."

When we had gotten to the top of the stairs, Eloise whispered again. "Just peek real quick, and run on in the bathroom like you're in a big hurry."

I turned to her frantically. "Aren't you coming, too?" She had led me to the top of the stairs and now she was going to desert me, leave me to do all the peeking and pretending.

"Oh, don't be such a scaredy-cat," and she gave me a push that sent me stumbling over the top stair and into the hall. Behind me, I heard Eloise running back down the stairs, giggling. She was a traitor and I hated her, and whatever I saw I would never tell her. But what I saw made me even more furious than I already was, even with all my resentment against Eloise for deserting me. For Whitey, big, ugly Whitey, was sitting comfortably in one of Mrs. O'Malley's chairs and smiling up at her.

"Aw, come on, baby," I heard him say in that startled moment when I stumbled over the top stair, and then I saw him tug vehemently at her arm and draw her down on his lap. What Mrs. O'Malley did or said I do not recall. All I know is that I rushed at him, fury in my heart and anger on my hand when I slapped his face. If Laddie had been with me, he would have killed Whitey. Mrs. O'Malley sometimes let *him* sit on her lap, and he loved to be petted and stroked by her as she fed him marshmallows and pieces of cake.

"You let her alone, you!" I shouted. "Quit hurting her."

Whitey was so amazed at this attack that he got abruptly up from the chair, almost tumbling Mrs. O'Malley onto the floor as he did so.

"Damn brat," he snarled, and I think he was going to strike me, but Mrs. O'Malley folded me into her arms, comforting me as I began to cry. Whitey picked up his empty tongs and strode out of the room, and I kicked at his shins as he passed me. The slap and the kick were to make up for all the injustice Mrs. O'Malley had suffered at the hands of these awful men, the unknown Mr. O'Malley, furtive Mr. Miller, and ugly, growling Whitey.

"I fixed him," I gulped finally, as I drew away from Mrs. O'Malley's soft, caressing arms. "I fixed him for hurting you."

Mrs. O'Malley looked out of the open French window, through which we could see the big white ice wagon lumbering down the street, a little faster then usual.

"Yes," Mrs. O'Malley replied slowly, a bit pensively. "You fixed him."

It was during her summer vacation that Mrs. O'Malley, time hanging heavy on her dainty little white hands, started coming to the library. She stared rather helplessly at first at the rows and rows of books, and thumbed somewhat aimlessly through a few of the magazines. (My sisters and I could have informed Mother that the magazines Mrs. O'Malley really enjoyed were *True Story* and numerous movie magazines, but since Mrs. O'Malley sometimes shared these fascinating and forbidden materials with us, we had no intention of ratting on her.) The clipping department was in an area toward the rear of the library, where not too many persons browsed. Mrs. O'Malley had wandered back there at a time when Mother was describing proudly to Mr. Bartholomew, a handsome young lawyer and frequent user of the library, the way she had organized the thousands of clippings—"something there to please everybody." Finally she had to leave Mr. Bartholomew to go about her other duties, but he assured her he could easily find what he was after, everything was so well organized.

"And maybe I can help," Mrs. O'Malley said softly. "Just think, *thousands* of clippings. Isn't it wonderful?"

"It—certainly—is," answered Mr. Bartholomew, staring at her appreciatively. "Just *wonderful.*"

Mother knew well that children who might not otherwise be readers were brought into libraries by story hours; indifferent students sent in by teachers to hunt up material for themes sometimes developed the library habit and even became true scholars. One never knew what might start a person on the road to reading. With Mrs. O'Malley, it seemed as though the clippings might have developed in her a passion for learning that she never knew she possessed. Mrs. O'Malley's childhood might have been deprived intellectually, Mother reasoned. Not everyone was fortunate enough to live in a town that had a free public library, or to grow up, as she had, in a family that realized the importance of books in a child's development. But it wasn't only Mrs. O'Malley who seemed enchanted with those thousands of clippings. When men like Mr. Leber and Mr. Miller and Mr. Troutman and Mr. Harrington—none of whom, as far as Mother was aware, had ever before set foot in the library—began using the clipping department, Mother felt she had finally reached the hard core, the unreachables. It was true Mr. Miller read only about fishing, but someday he might actually want to read Izaak Walton. Mr. Troutman, who favored astrology, might at some further period progress toward astronomy.

Even after her vacation ended, Mrs. O'Malley still kept coming to the library, and Mother regarded her as fondly as a minister might a non-believer who had finally begun to attend church regularly. She was actually a help to Mother, she knew so much about the clippings, and when she was there she was always happy to help a patron search for the information he wanted in the files. The clipping service had become so popular that a columnist for the local paper even wrote a story about it. It ran in the *Moberly Monitor-Index* the day before the really big story of the year, one that did not appear in the newspaper, broke. This was the scandal about Mrs. O'Malley and Mr. Leber.

Mrs. O'Malley left our apartment suddenly one Sunday in September. She came downstairs early in the morning to tell Mother she was moving. It was unbelievable; Mrs. O'Malley, pretty Mrs. O'Malley, sweet, quiet Mrs. O'Malley, was going to move.

"Oh, Mrs. O'Malley," Mother protested. "What's wrong? Were you worrying about your living room paper?"

"It's Mr. O'Malley," Mrs. O'Malley said softly. "He wants me to come back to him. I got a letter from him yesterday."

"Don't go," I cried out. "Just don't go."

"You'd better think twice," Mother said sagely. "If he left you once, he'll do it again."

Little Mrs. O'Malley blushed, but she was sweetly decided. She had to go, really she did. "Dear Mrs. Elsea, you've been so kind, and your three darling children." I think all of us were crying when, at noon, Mrs. O'Malley drove away in a taxicab to the station.

"I'll never have another roomer like her," Mother kept saying. "They don't come like that often, quiet, easy to please, and never late with the rent. And just when she'd gotten interested in the library."

As the taxicab bumped away down Logan Street, Mrs. Watkins, who lived across the street, came running over. "I see you found out all right," she said excitedly. "You certainly did put her out, bag and baggage."

"Found out what?" Mother asked, a little impatiently. For Mother was worried. There was the unpleasant business of renting the apartment again, of putting the ad in the paper, of waiting anxiously for the prospective renters to come, of trying to pick out someone good and respectable, and yet of trying to get someone as quickly as possible, so she would not lose any rent.

"I told Joe this morning that's what you'd do. I said to him, 'Carrie Elsea won't let anyone like that stay at her house.' But how'd you find out? I was coming over to tell you, and Joe kept saying, 'You mind your own business.'"

"What in the world are you talking about, Pearl Watkins?" Mother asked, bewildered now, as well as impatient.

"About Mrs. O'Malley and Mr. Leber," Mrs. Watkins said, surprised. "And about how Mrs. Leber took a whip to them both, and near tore both of them to ribbons."

Mother ran to the foot of the stairs and looked up as though she halfway expected Mrs. O'Malley to be coming down them. Then she sat down heavily, her hand held to her heart.

"You girls run outdoors and play," she said finally, and we ran from the room, not minding, because we knew we would stand at the kitchen door and hear everything said.

"She carried on with Herb Leber," Mrs. Watkins said, as soon as Eloise and Helen and I had gone out of the room.

"What did she do with Mr. Leber?" I whispered to Helen. "What did she carry?"

"Hush up," Helen whispered fiercely.

"It wasn't only Mr. Leber, either, it was Mr. Miller or Mr. Troutman or Mr. Ramsey, or any man. She always met them in the library, you know. Come to think of it," and Mrs. Watkins grew reflective, "I even saw her talking to Joe one day down on the corner, but didn't think anything of it at the time."

"She was such a sweet little woman," Mother said defensively. It wasn't only Mrs. O'Malley on trial, it was her apartment, and it was the library.

"Sweet on men," Mrs. Watkins sniffed. "Only Mrs. Leber found out about her honeying up to Herb Leber. She was hiding in the back of the car when Herb and Mrs. O'Malley came out of the library together last night, and when they were out on the Six Mile Lane she raised up from the back and made them get out of the car and began to hit at them with a big whip."

"A whip?" Mother's voice was shaky and terrible. "Where'd she get a whip?"

"Lord knows," said Mrs. Watkins. "Someone said it was an old buggy whip, and they'd seen it in Mildred Leber's garage."

I began to sniffle.

"Shut up," Helen said again ungraciously, and Eloise glared at me, furious. But I couldn't help it. I could see big cross-looking Mrs. Leber suddenly rising up from the back of Mr. Leber's car, brandishing a black whip and hitting at poor little Mrs. O'Malley, the wicked witch catching the good fairy. Mrs. O'Malley was gone away, I would never again hear her soft, tinkling laugh, never again be called a sweet little angel, the way she was always calling me, and she had been beaten by a big black whip.

"Now you've done it, you baby," Eloise said angrily. Mother had heard my sniffles and had opened the kitchen door to find us standing there.

"They'll find out about it sooner or later," Mrs. Watkins said sensibly. "Might as well let them know right now before any smart aleck tells them."

"Mrs. O'Malley's face was all red this morning, like she'd been crying," Helen said importantly. "And she walked like she didn't feel good."

"Why didn't Mrs. Leber want Mr. Leber to bring Mrs. O'Malley home in his car?" I asked, still sniffling. "People are always bringing us home from places."

"Oh, you little dummy," Helen said, disgustedly.

"I am not a dummy, I am not, I am not," and I flew at Helen with clenched fists.

"Stop that!" Mother admonished wearily. "What's the matter with you?"

"I don't care," and I burst out crying again. "You all leave her alone."

"Leave who alone, what are you talking about, for heaven's sake?"

"Mrs. O'Malley," I gulped, between sobs. "Everybody hurting her, Mrs. Leber and Whitey and Mr. Miller."

"What do you know about Mr. Miller?" Mother asked, and her voice had a terrible sound in it. "And who is Whitey?"

"Whitey's the iceman," Eloise said. "He took ice

up to Mrs. O'Malley."

"He jerked at her arm, real hard; he kept pulling and hurting her," I said, remembering with pleasure the way I had kicked Whitey's shins.

"We were trying to see what he did upstairs so long every day when he took up the ice," Eloise explained.

"Oh, God," Mother said, but it was not cursing, she was really invoking the help of the Lord. "In my own house, carrying on in my own house."

"Even the iceman," Mrs. Watkins said solemnly.

"There he is now," Eloise said. "There's the ice wagon out in front right now."

Mother ran to the front door.

"No ice today," she called out angrily.

Mrs. Watkins stood behind Mother, staring curiously at Whitey, and Helen and Eloise and I poked out our heads from behind them. Whitey stood on the front walk helplessly for a moment, the ice that he carried in his tongs dripping around his feet. Then he gave a bewildered look toward the upstairs French window, where no little white hand fluttered, where no soft red hair shone in the sunlight, and he turned and walked slowly back to his ice wagon. Laddie, who was out in the yard, followed him a little way, as though he were considering biting him, but Whitey seemed so dejected that he probably thought it was not worth the effort. Also, he knew from painful experience that a block of ice swung from a pair of tongs could be a powerful weapon.

Mr. Troutman and Mr. Miller suddenly became indifferent to the clipping collection. So did a great many other gentlemen who had patronized it so enthusiastically. But by now Mother knew that Mr. Miller would never have graduated to Izaak Walton, and that Mr. Troutman was incapable of rising above horoscopes. As for Mr. Leber, I have a feeling he would never again see an automobile without awaiting the lash of a whip whirring about his shoulders, and remembering the sweet little redhead who had helped him find out all about cars in the wonderful clipping collection at Mr. Carnegie's Lib'ary.

4

FAIR OPHELIA

I always knew that if I had to marry Mr. Carnegie or Mr. Shakespeare, I would choose Mr. Carnegie. The subject of marriage was uppermost in the minds of my circle of girl friends in school when we played "London Bridge Is Falling Down" at recess. When London Bridge fell on my fair lady, she was always asked such puzzlers as "Which would you rather have, a solid gold bathtub or a silver bed?" or "Who would you rather marry, John D. Rockefeller or Henry Ford?" I usually chose the golden bathtub, but I was not satisfied with either Mr. Rockefeller or Mr. Ford. To me, a better selection of husbands would be William Shakespeare and Andrew Carnegie.

Although both of these gentlemen were a vital part of the library, somehow Mr. Carnegie was cozier, and I felt I knew him better. It was true that his portrait did look cross, but so did Mr. Shakespeare's plaster bust, and no wonder, since both of the poor men were dead. Who wouldn't be mad as a hornet ending up as an oil painting or a plaster bust?

Mother, who considered the far-fetched problems I presented to her as seriously as I did, had difficulty making up her mind about these two hypothetical marriage partners.

"It would be a terrible decision," she admitted. She admired and was grateful to Mr. Carnegie, but she had revered Mr. Shakespeare ever since she had first been introduced to his work in college. She had actually *known* him twenty-five years longer than she had Mr. Carnegie.

Our living-room bookcase of black mission wood with glass doors was filled with Shakespeare's works. There was a fat, one-volume edition inscribed "To Caroline Eleanore Hutton, from Mama, Christman 1893–94"—Eloise and I, unknown to Mother, sometimes used it as a weight to press such things as letter flaps that would not stick—and a handsome twelve-volume set Mother had acquired in 1904. The flyleaves and margins of all these volumes were filled with lengthy notations, showing that Mother did not merely read Shakespeare, she studied him; when she did not understand a word, or did not know how to pronounce it, she looked it up and recorded it on the page.

"Thou cacodaemon!" proclaims Queen Margaret about the Duke of Gloucester in *King Richard III*.

Here was a new word to Mother. She had written in the pronunciation, "kak-o dé mon."

It was her twelve-volume set that showed her course of study through the years. "Finished Dec. 28, 1904, Clinton Shakespeare Club," she wrote at the end of *Romeo and Juliet*, and "Reread Oct., 1917." For some reason she did not get around to *Coriolanus* until September, 1916.

Just looking at Mother's set of Shakespeare always made me sleepy. There were so many books in the set, and when I did peek in them from time to time — always misled by the bright red binding with its gilt trim into thinking I would find something exciting there — I found Mr. Shakespeare's language almost unintelligible.

"Oh place and greatness! millions of false eyes
Are stuck upon thee. Volumes of report
Run with base, false and most contrarious quests
Upon thy doings . . ."

Why in the world, if he was such a great writer, didn't he make sense?

Mother was disappointed that neither Helen nor Eloise nor I had a taste for Shakespeare. We all preferred to sit in front of the shiny, new Victrola, listen to sad songs, and cry. One song in particular, "All Alone, I'm So All Alone," gave us a masochistic pleasure. We were always hopeful for "a ring, a ding-a-ling" from various boys, a ding-a-ling that often never came. Although at my age nobody but girls called me, there was forever the possibility that a boy in my class, whom I secretly admired almost as much as Mr. Carnegie and Mr. Shakespeare, would someday telephone. He was nicknamed Egg, since his father owned a company that sold chickens and eggs, and I had written several times in my tablet, "Mrs. Egg Carter," thinking it looked as impressive as Mrs. Andrew Carnegie and Mrs. William Shakespeare. And Egg was easier to cry over because I could see him every day at school—his teeth gleaming with gold braces—and could grieve at his indifference.

"Here you sit, listening by the hour to these ordinary songs, when right at your elbow is the greatest writer in English literature," Mother complained when she found us by the Victrola sighing and weeping over disappointed love. Mr. Carnegie would never have chosen one of us for his wife, Mother knew. She had read that he used a verse from Shakespeare in his selection of a mate, and that he had advised young men to apply the same test before offering themselves.

". . . For several virtues
Have I lik'd several women," mused both Ferdinand in *The Tempest*, and Mr. Carnegie in considering his bride-to-be.

". . . never any
With so full soul, but some defect in her
Did quarrel with the noblest grace she ow'd,
And put it to the foil.
"But you, O you!" they both finally caroled,

Ferdinand to Miranda, and Mr. Carnegie to his beloved:

"So perfect and so peerless, are created

Of every creature's best."

Although we were not perfect and peerless, we were good girls anyway, Mother admitted loyally, even if we were silly, and she only hoped some young men would come along who did not know about Mr. Carnegie's test for brides.

The only thing about our distaste for reading Shakespeare that comforted Mother was the fact that most of the members of her Shakespeare Club admitted that their children did not read him either. Mother had belonged to a Shakespeare Club for many years, first in Clinton, Missouri, where she had spent most of her married life, and then in her home town of Moberly, to which she returned after my father's death.

Moberly, like Mother, believed in culture. By 1904, when Mr. Carnegie's Lib'ary opened for business, Mr. Shakespeare was already established in Moberly. Although he arrived officially with the Shakespeare Club in 1897, certainly he had been there even earlier, since he had become a part of Mother's life, as her first Shakespeare volume indicated, in 1893. For all I know, he was a part of the very first library in Moberly—it lasted only three years—which was opened in November of 1872 by the Moberly Library Association, with 335 books and eight magazines. All you had to have to read them was five dollars a year for membership. I am practically sure that Shakespeare was represented in the Railroad Employees Library Club, the second group to attempt the establishment of a permanent library—it, too, was abandoned—and I am confident he was safely ensconced in the public library supported by town funds that opened on August 1, 1901, in the two rooms of the Railroad Library Club on Main Street. As a young girl, Mother had seen Shakespeare's plays presented in Hegarty's Opera House by home talent groups under the sponsorship of the Railroad Literary Club, as well as by professional, big-time actors, and she had known the Moberly girl who, fittingly enough, became the wife of the great Shakespearean actor Otis Skinner.

Mother knew very well that many people who came into the library said they read Shakespeare when they did not. She realized he was not everyone's cup of tea. The only persons she was sure of were the Shakespeare Club members. It was a great pity that people did not realize what romance and wisdom—even gore if they wanted it—were in the pages of Mr. Shakespeare's works.

"Now just listen to this, girls," she would say excitedly, looking up from *A Midsummer Night's Dream*, which she was rereading for probably the tenth time.

"O Sisters Three,
   Come, come to me,

With hands as pale as milk;
Lay them in gore,
Since you have shore
With shears, his thread of silk."

I am sure she thought this would stir us, since we were sisters three, but her outburst only embarrassed us. Most mothers we knew did not talk about hands as pale as milk. I only sighed sadly. My hands were not milk-white at all, but sunburned and freckle-spotted, and sometimes I bit my nails. Nonetheless, I would not want to lay them in gore.

If her own daughters, surrounded as they were by Shakespeare, were so indifferent to him, what could one expect of the rest of the town — of the country — Mother wondered. Mr. Carnegie, who loved Shakespeare as much as Mother did, must have worried about this state of affairs, too, and had somehow gotten a message through to Mother, because one day she came up with the idea for one of her finest library displays of all time. It was entitled "Mr. Carnegie Read Shakespeare — Why Don't You?"

Momentarily Mr. Carnegie's portrait came down from the wall in the entry and went up over the Shakespeare-Carnegie display, next to William Shakespeare's bust. Both of them looked a bit merry in each other's company, Mr. Carnegie admiring culture as he did, and Mr. Shakespeare appreciating a rich patron. Mother displayed all of the library's volumes of Shakespeare, as well as Mr. Carnegie's own autobiography, opened to the page where he told of his discovery of Shakespeare. As a youth of fifteen, Mr. Carnegie delivered telegrams to the Pittsburgh Theater, and was given a free seat for a performance of one of Shakespeare's plays.

"Thenceforth there was nothing for me but Shakespeare," he remembered in the story of his life. Mother printed this over Mr. Carnegie's portrait.

"Just think," she said accusingly to Eloise and Helen and me, "Andrew Carnegie was only *fifteen* when he felt this way about Shakespeare."

I was only twelve at this time, but I had had intellectual advantages that Andrew Carnegie, a very poor boy, had not, so I was not exempt from her scorn. I had been exposed to Shakespeare in my home from the minute I was born. (I would not be surprised if Mother had been deep in *As You Like It* or *Hamlet* right up to the moment of my birth, and jotting notes on the margins of the pages.) Also, since I had taken elocution lessons from the time I was eight years old, Mother felt I might try to emulate Mr. Carnegie, who could declaim whole scenes from Shakespeare, and even at times, whole plays.

The quote from Mr. Carnegie that pleased Mother the most was one he was supposed to have remarked to a friend when William H. Vanderbilt passed by — "I would not exchange his millions for my knowledge of Shakespeare." She printed this in big letters for the display, knowing full well that this was a direct slap at some of the town citizens who were too busy making money to bother with the library.

Certainly there was no reason for anyone in Moberly who had eyes in his head not to know a little something about William Shakespeare, as well as Moberly's cultural benefactor, Andrew Carnegie. The Shakespeare-Carnegie display was there for all to see. Mother had read somewhere that Mr. Carnegie, during a sea voyage of two weeks, read fourteen of Shakespeare's plays and noted in his diary passages that other famous poets had pirated from Shakespeare. If Mr. Carnegie could read fourteen plays in two weeks, and he as busy as he was, even on an ocean voyage, every person in Moberly could read at least one play once a year.

Mother found a picture of Mr. Shakespeare's home in Stratford-on-Avon and one of Anne Hathaway's cottage. She also arranged a photograph of Mr. Carnegie's shabby but historic little birthplace in Dunfermline, Scotland, alongside one of turreted Skibo castle in Scotland, which he purchased when he was a millionaire. Skibo was located near Macbeth's castle and the hill of Dunsinane, as was only right and proper.

"If ever a boy deserved to live in a castle when he grew up, Andrew Carnegie did," Mother said admiringly. "Just look where he came from."

These contrasting pictures of Mr. Carnegie's homes, Mother felt, should inspire any poor boy in

Moberly to seek to better himself in the world. And one of the best ways to start was to come into the library and check out Shakespeare. While he was there, the boy might notice for further inspiration a quotation of Mr. Carnegie's that Mother kept permanently and prominently displayed on the circulation desk: "The poorest labourer in the district with his wife and children march into this library, and are members of the highest society of all the world, without money and without price."

There was a run on Shakespeare for a while, and one lady in town who had recently seen Shakespeare's house in Stratford-on-Avon was in much demand as a speaker at the women's literary clubs. Many of the schoolteachers made their pupils write themes about Shakespeare, although there were a few reports that some parents felt parts of Shakespeare were dirty, even if he was so great. When she heard this, Mother said tartly, "Well, think of what's in the Bible."

Since I had memorized many a Bible verse in Sunday School contests, and had even won a Bible for my zeal in reciting, I myself had once come across a terrible verse that I would not utter in front of Mother. It was worse, even, than the part about Samson tying the tails of 300 foxes together and then setting them on fire, which was just plain mean. I had mentioned the terrible verse to my Sunday School teacher, who had replied crossly that she sometimes wondered if God had intended those particular lines to be included in His Book, and that I should forget them, as God Himself would have advised. I should have stuck with such folk as Noah, and David and Goliath, or Daniel in the lions' den, as she had told me to.

There was one unpleasant incident while the Shakespeare-Carnegie material was being featured. A crotchety old gentleman came up to Mother, pointed to the display, and asked, "What about the *real* Shakespeare?"

"The real Shakespeare?"

"The only man in the world who could have written those immortal plays and sonnets — Francis Bacon, Lord Verulam, the greatest man the world has ever known. Where's Francis Bacon's picture in all this, I'd like to know?"

Mother was aware that Shakespeare-Was-Really-Bacon believers existed; she also realized that they were wrong. Nevertheless, a library should try to present all facets of a subject without censorship, as long as they were decent, and the Bacon-Shakespeare people were decent, even though they were misguided. So a picture of Francis Bacon labeled "Was He Shakespeare?" and a few clippings on the subject also went up in a corner of the display. The Shakespeare Club members grumbled a bit at this heresy, and the ghosts of Mr. Carnegie and the real Mr. Shakespeare probably thought she was out of her mind, but Mother did not want anyone to think she was not absolutely fair.

Ultimately Mr. Carnegie went back on the wall over the entryway, Mr. Shakespeare went back on the library shelves, and the pictures of Stratford-on-Avon, Mr. Carnegie's homes, and Francis Bacon returned to the clipping file.

"Carrie, you try so *hard*," I heard one of the Shakespeare Club members say to Mother as the display was being dismantled—the Shakespeare Club members had generously lent some of their own Shakespeare mementos for the occasion—"although you know very well that you can lead a horse to water but you can't make him drink."

"Push his head down into the trough, then," Mother replied. "If he only gets his head wet, it's better than nothing."

And there was no doubt that a few of the library patrons had at least gotten their heads wet as a result of the Shakespeare display. Circulation reports showed Shakespeare had been for a while in several homes, even if he never got read. Mr. Carnegie's autobiography got checked out, too.

Of her three daughters, I was the one selected by Mother as most likely to reap the rewards of my cultural heritage. I was the most avid reader, I liked to draw, and to write compositions, I longed to be able to toe dance, and I took my elocution lessons very seriously. Surely I would turn out to be something in the world of art and literature. I was much in demand at church and school performances as a deliverer of "readings," and thus it was only natural and sensible that I should receive one of the leading parts in the eighth grade play — most of my friends were only Feathers or Cherry Blossoms or Butterflies. I portrayed a Japanese girl named San Fan, and Mother made me an elaborate kimono so that I would look correct for the part, even painting huge golden flowers on the material.

The acting was up to me. If I had not learned enough to comport myself on stage in a creditable fashion after four years of reciting, there was nothing more she could do. She even allowed me to get a marcel, and although we both knew this did not make me look Japanese, it did make me look prettier.

"People like to see pretty girls up on a stage," Mother observed wisely. "They already know very well you're not Japanese."

She was realistically aware that I had mouse-colored hair, a turned-up nose, and was small for my age, but she was hopeful that my voice, practically professional from years of training in elocution, would make me successful in my part. The fancy blue and gold hand-painted kimono would also help.

The women in Mother's Shakespeare Club turned out loyally to see the actress daughter of their sister member. It was, after all, one of the unwritten laws of club members to support each other in such ways. If they did not, who would attend the numerous piano recitals, elocution readings, graduations, and other important family occasions which the public had a tendency to ignore?

I was dutifully congratulated after my performance by each member, and one of Mother's cronies even went so far as to remark thoughtfully to Mother that she would not be surprised if I ended up being a Shakespearean actress. This naturally was enough to make any girl preen a bit, but the compliment that really mattered was the one given me by Mr. Lowell Whitlow, the handsome son of one of the members—he was nicknamed Lady Killer because of his many feminine conquests—who had accompanied his mother to the play. He stared at me lazily as I stood beside Mother receiving my compliments, and then, after the ladies finished their praise, he said firmly: "She will act the part of fair Ophelia on Broadway, or I'll miss my bet."

This from Lady Killer Lowell Whitlow himself! He was so magnificent to look at that all I could do, in spite of my newly acquired sophistication as an actress, was blush and bow my head in confusion. Lady Killer Lowell was quite old, at least twenty, and when a girl went out with him, her reputation, Helen and Eloise said, was likely to be left in shreds. It was well known that he collected girls' garters, but no matter what a girl said about him in private, if she were asked by him for a date, she went—and wore her prettiest garters, too.

"Fair Ophelia, the fairest of the fair," Lady

Killer murmured now, and he even smiled a wicked, thrilling smile before he left the auditorium with his mother, leaving me conscious of the fact that I was wearing a pair of tacky pink elastic roll garters instead of the frilled satin and lace kind that Lady Killer so admired.

"Which of Shakespeare's plays is fair Ophelia in?" I asked Mother eagerly, when we were walking home.

"You'll have to look it up yourself," Mother said unfeelingly. "If you want to know, you'll have to learn your Shakespeare, just as I did."

And then she said, puzzled, almost to herself, "I wonder what made him say *Ophelia*?"

I had to read through three volumes of Shakespeare before I found fair Ophelia in *Hamlet*. By then, however, I had discovered that it was like eating olives; once I got the taste for Shakespeare, I could not stop, even though I could not understand a great deal of what I was reading. I certainly could not figure out why Hamlet wanted poor Ophelia to go to a nunnery.

I still thought Mr. Carnegie was cozier than Mr. Shakespeare, but now, with more maturity, I realized if I *had* to marry either of them, I would choose Mr. Shakespeare, so that I could act in his plays.

Helen and Eloise never did change their minds about Shakespeare, though. It made them furious when they were trying to listen to and cry over

"Nobody's Sweetheart," that they had to hear me proclaiming, like Mr. Carnegie, whole scenes from Shakespeare, although I never quite mastered a whole play. They felt I was making fun of them when I intoned:

"Love is merely a madness, and, I tell you, deserves as well a dark house, and a whip, as madmen do."

Or, "This way will I take upon me to wash your liver as clean as a sound sheep's heart, that there shall not be one spot of love in it."

But Mother was delighted. Now when she would burst out:

"The pleasant'st angling is to see the fish
    Cut with her golden oars the silver stream,
    And greedily devour the treacherous bait:"

I would chime in:

"So angle we for Beatrice; who even now
    Is couched in the woodbine coverture."

Lady Killer Whitlow might never collect one of my garters, but there was a good chance he would some day see me acting Shakespeare on Broadway. And in order of their importance in my life, four names were scribbled now all over my notebook: William Shakespeare, Andrew Carnegie, Lowell Whitlow, Egg Carter.

5

THE BLASPHEMERS

"Andrew Carnegie would have had a fit," Mother said, after the Billupses acted up the way they did in the library. Right under his very nose, too—under his portrait, that is—Mrs. Billups screaming and carrying on like a wild woman. "For all I know," Mother added skeptically, "there may never have been a teacher's certificate in that trunk at all."

It was the teacher's certificate that had first endeared Mrs. Billups to Mother when the Billupses rented our apartment, since nothing was more respectable in Mother's eyes than a schoolteacher.

Mr. Billups was proud of Mrs. Billups' teacher's certificate, too. "It's right there in that trunk," he would say proudly, pointing to the huge black trunk covered with a fringed shawl that took up too much space in their living room. "She could go right out and teach in any school in Missouri with that certificate back of her."

Not that Mrs. Billups ever had made any use of her certificate. She had never taught anything in her life, but the idea that she could if she took a notion fascinated her husband. There, safe in the trunk, was a fine wonderful career that never had its birth because Mrs. Billups had chosen him instead. I think he felt the pride of a man who had snatched a woman from the arms of an important rival and knew everyone in town was thinking how lucky he was.

Mrs. Billups would just smile a lazy, tolerant smile when Mr. Billups mentioned her certificate, and I am sure that even though she might have worked to get the paper, she never had the slightest intention of using it, never had the faintest desire to teach a roomful of children the Palmer method (your hand is a turtle, children, coming out of its shell, push, pull, push, pull), or get white chalk dust over her beautiful black satin dresses. Perhaps Mrs. Billups had only one black satin dress, but it seemed as though she had a great many of them, because one day there would be a flaming red velvet rose at the waist of the satin, and another day a handful of white chiffon would be draped about the collar.

Mrs. Billups was very tall and had wonderful yellow hair that she draped in folds and braids and curls around her lovely head. I used to imagine how it must be to have hair like that, soft yellow silk lying in sun. I would run my hands through my straight brown hair, trying to bind it into smooth braids, or spit on my bangs and curl them patiently against my forehead, wet and straight and gluey looking.

Mrs. Billups looked soft and shining and elegant even when she did her housework, but she did not do much work at all. Mostly she sat and listened to phonograph records. There was one that she played over and over until we got so tired of hearing it that we wished it would break in two, but the tune ran in our minds, unwanted, unforgettable, with its plaintive lament for "My Buddy."

"My Buddy, my Buddy, your Buddy misses you. . . ."

On and on the record played, over and over.

"My God, don't it ever run down?" Mr. Billups asked her one day. But Mrs. Billups just laughed softly and went over to the phonograph and began to play the record again.

"She must have had a buddy she loved," Helen said knowingly. "He must have died or something."

I could see in my mind Mrs. Billups, sad and beautiful and weeping, standing beside the tomb of her dead buddy, wearing one of her black satin dresses and singing "Your buddy misses you," with crying in her voice and a little hiccup at the end like the girl singing on the record.

The empty lot next to our house was adjacent to a narrow side street that was as dark and quiet at night as the lot itself. Early in the evening the lot was filled with noise, because most of the neighborhood children played there. All over the block one could hear the shrill, piercing calls of "Run, sheep, run," or the sharp command, "White Rabbit," which meant stop where you are and if you move a finger you'll be called in, you'll be out of the game. Later at night the lot belonged to the darkness and quiet, and to unseen, imagined things.

"Where's your sash?" Eloise asked me one night when I came in from playing on the lot. "Your dress is hanging like a sack." I felt my waist. Eloise was right, my sash was gone, and my dress was hanging lank and shapeless. I ran, a little fearfully, back to the lot and searched around by the big tree, but I soon tired of groping around in the dark for an old sash. And besides, I was frightened. One morning we had found some broken whiskey bottles in the big hole in the middle of the lot where our house used to stand.

"Drunk men have been here," Helen said solemnly. "Drunk men on this very lot."

So always at night I thought of those men hiding in the deep hole or behind bushes, men with shaggy beards and dirty clothes and red eyes, like a man whom I had once seen drunk. Even worse, Eloise said that ghosts of the people who used to live in our house still haunted the spot where their house used to be.

All of a sudden I thought I heard a soft laugh at the far end of the lot on the terrace by the street, the part we called the grove, because of the bushes and trees which formed a sort of shelter. Some of my friends might still be lingering about, and even though I myself was frightened I decided to creep up on them down there in the grove and scare the daylights out of them. I moved silently down the weedy lot, but as I came up to the grove and started to give a loud scream and jump out, I realized these weren't my friends at all. They were two grownups, standing over by the bushes. The woman spoke, huskily. It was Mrs. Billups' voice.

"He doesn't get in tonight, does he?" another voice asked.

"No, not until tomorrow afternoon," Mrs. Billups said dreamily. "His train doesn't get in until around four o'clock."

"Hell, we got all the time in the world," the rough voice went on.

Mrs. Billups only laughed again, but it was a funny little laugh, as though she'd caught a cold.

I wished I could see who Mrs. Billups was with, but all I could see was a big black shape. They didn't say anything at all then for a few moments, and I was disappointed, thinking they might have gone away and that I was staring only at bushes.

"Buddy," Mrs. Billups said suddenly and sharply, "Buddy!"

No one answered her and she didn't speak again, either. So, after a couple of minutes I crawled silently away, thinking I'd heard everything that was going to be said. It was no fun watching something you couldn't really see. I was excited, though, and felt strange inside. Because that was Mrs. Billups' buddy, and he wasn't dead as Helen said he must be, he was a big black shape, and no one knew about him but Mrs. Billups and me.

Mrs. Billups seemed more mysterious and beautiful than ever when I saw her the next day. She was lying on the day bed knitting and listening to records while I sat on top of her big black trunk fingering the silk tassels of the shawl that covered it. She did not talk to me, though. Both of us just sat there without saying a word, she humming every once in a while with the record she was playing, and I in a blissful stage, content only to look at her lying on the day bed, beautiful and romantic, like a princess in a book. The room seemed shabby and not fine enough for her. She ought to be reclining on a pink satin bed, instead of the orange and brown cretonne-covered couch, and she should have huge fluffy satin pillows at her back, with her lovely yellow hair billowing against them. Mother's hand-painted pictures, the gypsy girl lying on the river bank, and the little windmill scene, and the picture of the mother holding a baby, which I had always been so proud of, seemed dull and shabby, too, and should instead have been paintings of dancing ladies with beautiful shawls, framed in a lot of sparkling gilt.

Finally Mrs. Billups put "My Buddy" on the phonograph, and she sang the words softly and dreamily under her breath, but they didn't seem sad the way she sang them. I felt I had to say something then, because after all I knew about Buddy now, there was a bond between Buddy and Mrs. Billups and me. I wanted to let her know I had seen Buddy, but I was afraid to tell her I had stood behind the bushes in the lot's darkness and listened to her talk to him.

"Helen says your buddy must be dead," I blurted out finally, hoping she would tell me all about him.

"What?" Mrs. Billups asked, as though she hadn't heard me.

"Your buddy, like on the Victrola—Helen says he must be dead."

Mrs. Billups looked at me with interest. "What makes her think that?"

"The piece is all so sad, and the girl cries in the end. So Helen says your buddy must have died."

"Poor Buddy," murmured Mrs. Billups.

"I don't think he's dead, though," I said bravely.

"Oh, he's been dead for a long while, quite dead," Mrs. Billups said, but she smiled as she said it, as though very amused at something, and I knew she was just joking with me. Buddy wasn't dead at all. He couldn't be, no matter what she said, because I had seen him, or rather I had heard him, last night.

That evening I went down to the library to walk home with Mother. Just as we were starting to close up the library we saw Mrs. Billups running up the stairs in the main entry. This in itself was unusual, because Mrs. Billups was not a reader. I had never before seen her in the library. But stranger still was the fact that she was stumbling and breathless, her yellow hair tumbling far below her shoulders, while Mr. Billups was racing up the stairs after her, shouting in a terrible voice. I could scarcely believe it was Mr. Billups, who was usually so gentle and adoring of his wife.

"He tried to choke me!" Mrs. Billups gasped. "He had me in the car outside trying to choke me!" And she fell against Mother, who stared at her in horror. This kind of thing just did not happen in the library. It was all a mistake, a dreadful mistake.

"Call the police!" Mrs. Billups went on wildly. "Have him locked up, I won't stay in the same house with him."

Mother looked around her frantically, grateful that there were no others but ourselves in the library at this time.

"I can't have this sort of thing happening *here*," Mother said over and over, as though she could scarcely believe she was seeing and hearing right. What were the Billupses thinking of, running into the library, of all places, with their shouts and their screams?

Mrs. Billups sat down on the steps, sobbing, and Mr. Billups must have suddenly gotten embarrassed about the whole thing, because he disappeared down the stairs and out the door.

I began to cry, too. "What are we going to do,

Mother, what are we going to do?"

"Quit your crying," Mother said sharply. "Get on your sweater. We'll call a taxi and go to the Nevinses'."

"Why are we going to the Nevinses'?" I asked, peering outside, hoping to see more of Mr. Billups.

"You don't think we're going to go home and maybe find *him* upstairs, do you?" Mother said quickly.

Mr. Nevins was our next-door neighbor and the rock to which our family clung when faced with small or large disasters. He was masterful and magnificent in times of distress. We depended on Mrs. Nevins, with her always well-stocked pantry, to rescue us from minor crises, such as running out of milk or eggs in the middle of mixing a cake or a pudding, but it was to Mr. Nevins we appealed piteously when the water pipes burst, or we thought we heard burglars, or something was wrong with the furnace. We four females were surely mill-stones around the neck of Mr. Nevins, and whenever he saw us running across the drive toward his house he must have thought, "*Again?*"—but at the same time felt strong and mighty and all-powerful in his ability to straighten things out for us. Mr. Nevins somehow suggested an entire tribe of fierce Celtic warriors from whom he was surely descended, the wild fighting Irish of pagan times who thought nothing of lopping off heads, chopping up enemies, and dragging captives through fearsome forests.

As our neighbor and our defender in times of threatened disaster, he represented terror to overwhelm terror. Also, he had three strong sons, as fierce, when occasion demanded, as their father.

The moment we arrived at the Nevinses' by taxi, all of the Nevinses, in fact all of the immediate neighbors, knew something awful had happened — for whoever rode in *taxis*, unless a great and unusual emergency had arisen?

"I can handle him," Mr. Nevins said angrily when he heard about Mr. Billups. Naturally we all knew he could; that was why we were there. "I'll go over and talk to him."

But Mrs. Billups was determined. "He's going to jail," she said. Her lovely eyes grew hard and glittering, and she was not the soft, smiling Mrs. Billups I knew at all. She looked strange with her hair all over her face and shoulders, tangled and wild and golden.

Mr. Nevins was his bravest and most efficient, calling the police, giving Mrs. Billups advice, and offering encouragement to Mother, who kept saying, "Why in the world did they have to come running into the *library*?" — just as though Mrs. Billups were not right there hearing every word she said about her. When two policemen arrived, Mr. Nevins even went with them into our house to seek out Mr. Billups, who was greatly insulted by their visit, and more insulted still when forced to accompany the policemen to jail for the night.

I was looking out of the Nevinses' window when Mr. Billups left our house with the policemen, and I felt sorry for poor Mr. Billups, and not afraid of him any more at all. He was not angry and red and ugly now, just confused, and he kept staring helplessly over at the Nevinses' house as he got into the car with the two policemen. Laddie had gotten mixed up about who the villain was and was barking madly at the policemen. I called to Mrs. Billups to tell her Mr. Billups was looking over this way, and did she want to peek out of the window and wave good-by to him, but she only turned away as though she had not heard me and stared off into space, quiet again, and half smiling.

The next day was one of confusion and excitement. Mr. Billups came home, looking very sheepish, and tried to get up the stairs without running into Mother, but that was impossible. Mother had been watching for him, determinedly watching, and when Mother watched for anyone that way, there was not the slightest chance that he could escape.

"You know, Mr. Billups, I won't tolerate affairs like the one last night," Mother said, looking at him so sternly that poor Mr. Billups lowered his head and stared around wildly for a way of escape from her.

"You'll have to move, of course," she continued. "Today. You must leave today."

"Today?" Mr. Billups gasped. "But we don't want to move, Mrs. Elsea, we like it here very much.

Last night was just a misunderstanding. Just a little misunderstanding."

"Of course it was," Mrs. Billups said. She had been standing at the top of the stairs, I guess, because now she came gracefully down the steps, smiling at Mr. Billups.

Mother was adamant. "Misunderstanding or what-not, you'll have to leave today."

Mrs. Billups looked at Mr. Billups, alarmed. Then she said anxiously to Mother, "Oh, we can't leave today, Mrs. Elsea. We really can't go."

"To think you would make a scene in the *library*," Mother just said again and again, still almost unbelieving. "Fighting and choking a woman almost to death and then coming into the *library*."

Mr. and Mrs. Billups gazed helplessly at each other, but Laddie, who by now was getting the villain identified in his shaggy brain, sensed Mother's mood, and was beginning to snarl and sniff unpleasantly at Mr. Billups' legs.

"I'll take your rent money now," Mother said determinedly. "You owe for two weeks."

Late in the afternoon, when Mr. Billups was getting his car out of the garage and piling boxes and suitcases and odds and ends that belonged to them in it, I spoke to Mrs. Billups for the last time. I stood around the top of the stairs, pretending I was hunting telephone numbers, but watching Mrs. Billups out of the corner of my eye, because her door was open. She was packing her dresses, folding them carefully and lovingly with tissue paper between them.

"Peggy," she called out softly.

I dropped the phone book and went dashing into her room. Mrs. Billups was holding the lovely red velvet flower that she wore at the waist of her black satin and was twisting it around and around in her fingers. She thrust the flower into my hand impulsively, and smiled. "You keep this. Wear it on your good dress, that little blue one I saw you wearing the other day and looking so pretty in."

I looked at the wonderful red flower in amazement, feeling its soft velvety petals and smelling the rich perfume that Mrs. Billups must have poured lavishly over it.

"If anyone should call me," Mrs. Billups went on quickly, glancing out into the hallway, "a man, perhaps, an old friend of mine, a—sort of a relative—will you tell him I'll get in touch with him right away to let him know where I am?"

I looked at her wide-eyed and knowingly. "Your buddy?" I asked hoarsely. "You mean your buddy?"

The real-life Buddy, I meant, of course. The Buddy on the record was gone forever, I knew. We had heard the piece briefly earlier in the day after Mr. Billups' return. The needle had gotten stuck in a ridge in the Victrola record, and we could hear a distracted voice from the phonograph pleading over and over, "My Buddy, my Buddy, my Buddy . . ." until suddenly there was a terrible smashing sound upstairs, and the music was gone.

Mrs. Billups gave a nervous little laugh. "Yes, my buddy, that's who it will be." She pressed the flower deeper into my hand. "You'll listen for the telephone this evening, won't you? And not say a word to anyone else about it."

The evening paper came just after the Billupses had moved out of the house. As Mother read it, she gave an awful cry that frightened Eloise and me.

"They didn't have to put in our address," Mother said angrily. "Just wait till I go down to the *Monitor-Index*, I'll give them a piece of my mind." I felt awfully sorry for the people at the *Moberly Monitor-Index*, because they were in for a terrible time if Mother planned to give them a piece of her troubled mind.

We looked at the sentence Mother had just been reading. "A. R. Billups, 406 West Logan, was arrested last night for disturbing the peace."

"Our address," Mother breathed. "They let everyone know that the Billupses lived at our house. The disgrace of it. Everybody in Thursday Club and Eastern Star will know. Thank God they didn't mention the library. But I could choke them for putting our address in."

Suddenly she looked puzzled. "I wonder why he did try to choke her," she said, almost to herself. It wasn't the *Monitor-Index* she was thinking about now, you could tell. "What in the world do you suppose ever made him act that way?"

"Her old records," Helen said. "I bet she played them and played them until he couldn't stand them. That piece she played all the time was broken in a million pieces. I saw it in the tin can box, smashed to bits. And I heard him say to her this afternoon that it was the fault of that Buddy person."

"My Buddy," Eloise explained to Mother. "The piece Mrs. Billups played all the time. I don't guess Mr. Billups liked it."

"A woman with a teacher's certificate," Mother puzzled, "to get mixed up with a thing like that." Then she added, "*if* she had a teacher's certificate."

The telephone rang. Usually none of us wanted to run up the long flight of stairs to answer it. "I'm not going," Helen said. "I said so first."

"Me neither," said Eloise quickly.

I didn't say a word, only ran toward the stairs to be sure I would get to answer it, while Eloise and Helen looked at me in amazement. My Buddy, the mysterious, the wonderful, the dark shape, the voice, would be waiting for me at the telephone. Only I in all the world had the secret message for him from the beautiful Mrs. Billups. It was no wonder that he and Mr. Billups and everyone loved her. She was so perfect that even Mr. Carnegie must have forgiven her for screaming under his very nose.

6
WOMAN OF SORROW

Mrs. Friedhoff, in all the time she frequented the library, read nothing but romances. As a rule Mother would secretly be extremely scornful of a library patron who had such limited reading habits. She liked quoting Montaigne, that "books of that sort ... were not able to charm me, even in my childhood." She even approved, in some cases, of Napoleon's terrible habit of throwing books that did not please him out the door or into the fire, or even out the windows of his carriage, although as a librarian, a preserver of books, she did not emulate him.

In Mrs. Friedhoff's case, however, Mother encouraged her light reading and saw that the newest love stories, tacky as they were, were saved for her as soon as they arrived in the library. First of all, Mrs. Friedhoff had been a high-school English teacher before her marriage, and thus she knew better than to think the trash she read was literature. And putting up with Mr. Friedhoff, Mother said privately to Grandmother, a few weeks after the Friedhoffs had moved upstairs to our apartment, made Mrs. Friedhoff deserving of any escape literature that she could lay her hands on. If the happy endings in trashy novels helped Mrs. Friedhoff to endure, then hurray for happy endings. Coming from Mother, who believed that one should always aim high in life and literature, this showed the measure of her affection and respect for Mrs. Friedhoff.

Actually, Mrs. Friedhoff did not have the time to read all of the romances she checked out, but it seemed to bolster her to have a pile of them around her, as though in some marvelous fashion the assorted heroes in the novels would at some time spring from the pages of the books to rescue her and her three children from her husband.

None of us, from Mother on down to Laddie, could endure Mr. Friedhoff. From the very beginning Laddie knew there was something not quite right about him. He was Enemy to Laddie from the first day the Friedhoffs set foot in our house, the scent of past wrongs and misdeeds strong on him, as far as Laddie was concerned.

Laddie did not bother with trivial tricks, such as sitting up to beg, playing dead, or jumping through hoops. He was occupied with the more important work of protecting his family by warding off door-to-door salesmen, gypsies, tramps, and any suspicious-looking creature who ventured near our house. But there was a quality about Mr. Friedhoff that Laddie could not fathom. His was not a forthright evil, as exemplified by tramps and trespassers, with whom Laddie knew well how to cope, simply by snarling and biting. He was the bravest dog in the world, as he and we all knew — except when it came to Mr. Friedhoff.

"Can't your pooch do anything?" Mr. Friedhoff asked the first day he saw Laddie. "Is he too dumb to learn tricks?"

Laddie eyed him insolently, looking as stupid as he could, his pink tongue hanging loosely from his mouth, his eyes glassy and cold.

"I'll teach that mutt to sit up and beg," Mr. Friedhoff said, and his eyes were glassy and cold, too, and determined.

Laddie was limp and unresponsive to Mr. Friedhoff's coaching. He did not know what "sit" meant, and he had no intention of learning.

At first Mr. Friedhoff coaxed him with crackers. "Sit up, hound," and Mr. Friedhoff's eyes grew harder each time Laddie fell limply to the floor after being pushed into a sitting position. Suddenly Mr. Friedhoff picked up the broom standing in the corner of the kitchen.

"Don't you hit him with that," Eloise screamed out, and I ran over to protect Laddie, whose eyes had a new hatred and terror in them.

Afterward Mr. Friedhoff swore it was an accident, the broom fell out of his hand, he had only meant to use it to prod Laddie gently. However it was meant, the broom fell with a whack on Laddie's back, he uttered a howl of protest and resentment— and he sat. And until the day of his death, twelve years later, it was his favorite trick, to be used when he was hungry, when he wanted out or in, when he wanted to be noticed. But he never forgave Mr. Friedhoff.

Mrs. Friedhoff was a woman of great sorrow, her own mother had told Mother. Eloise and Helen and I did not know what that meant. Mrs. Friedhoff looked just like anyone else to us. She talked and she laughed and she cooked and sewed, there was nothing about her that made her seem strange, like a woman of great sorrow. Maybe she did not like Mr. Friedhoff; this was the only thing we could think of.

The Friedhoffs had two little boys and a little girl. Looking back now, I can see that that alone would make for sorrow for Mrs. Friedhoff—five people living in our two-room-and-kitchenette apartment. The two boys slept in the big brass bed in the bedroom and little Nellilee in her baby bed, while Mr. and Mrs. Friedhoff slept on the studio couch in the living room.

We always knew when Mr. Friedhoff was coming down the street in the evening on his way home from work. We would hear Laddie whimpering at the door. When he got caught out on the porch or in the yard with none of us near to bring him in, we would see him crouch against the house or close to the ground, his tail between his legs, as Mr. Friedhoff passed by. But if Mr. Friedhoff called out "Sit," Laddie would sit up desperately, his eyes rolling around to us for help. It always seemed to please Mr. Friedhoff to have Laddie sit up for him. The trick was a product of his power, the dog obeyed his will; the dog hated him, but he obeyed.

I think his whole family responded to him as Laddie did. I know the little boys were in terror of him most of the time. I had heard him, at night, whipping them, and had heard Mrs. Friedhoff's gentle, agonized little voice remonstrating, "Harry, Harry, please, not so hard." But Mr. Friedhoff never seemed to hear her. The next day the little boys would charge a penny to look at their bruises.

"Look at that, big as a dollar," Benny would say, exposing a blue, bruise-spotted shoulder. They were very bold and brave all day, Benny and Herbert Friedhoff, but late in the afternoon when it was time for their father to come home, they usually got quiet and stopped playing, and if Mrs. Friedhoff called them they would go in the house without a word of protest.

The first time I was aware of death as being close and presenting a threat even to me, the immortal, was when the Friedhoffs lived at our house. Creeping up the stairs, although I had been told not to, I peered into the Friedhoff's bedroom, and death was there in the big brass bed, death and crying and the smell of medicine. Mrs. Friedhoff was sitting in a chair by the bed, her face pale and strange, with hate and tightness in it, staring at Mr. Friedhoff who stood by the bed.

"That's the way Laddie looks at him," I thought suddenly, this thought larger and clearer to me than death. But I was afraid to look in any longer. I crept silently down the stairs.

"The hearse just came," Eloise whispered. "Watch out, the hearse will get you."

But it wouldn't get me, either. Laddie and I ran out the back door and over into the empty lot, into the little grove at the back. We stayed there until the hearse had gone and still we did not want to go home. I wished I had not seen little Nellilee lying on the big brass bed, and the terrible way Mrs. Friedhoff had looked at Mr. Friedhoff.

Nellilee was only three when the Friedhoffs moved to our house. "But she's a good child and very quiet," Mrs. Friedhoff had said anxiously the day they came to look at our apartment.

Like all landladies, Mother did not like to rent to people with children, little Indians to pencil and crayon the wallpaper and abuse the furniture. I don't know what made Mother take the Friedhoffs. Perhaps it was the desperate, pathetic way Mrs. Friedhoff looked at her when she said the children would be no trouble, or maybe Mother was remembering her own three children and what she would have done if she had had to search for an apartment and landladies had turned us away. Anyway, Mrs. Friedhoff was right about Nellilee. She was a good, quiet child. She was with Mrs. Friedhoff most of the time, following her about, staring gravely at people who came in. The little boys were usually outside playing, wild noisy little animals, but Nellilee was her mother's child.

Mrs. Friedhoff talked to her all day long.

"Now we've got to do the washing, Nellilee," or "I guess we'll take the garbage downstairs."

Neither of them laughed much, but they often smiled at each other, a sort of secret, understanding smile when there was nothing at all to smile about. Sometimes Mrs. Friedhoff would even read part of one of her romances out loud to Nellilee, who did not understand it, but knew from the way her mother read to her that it was a wonderful story that always ended happily.

One day Nellilee had a big fever blister on her upper lip and she smelled like camphor. Mr. Fried-hoff would not kiss her when he saw it. For some peculiar reason Mr. Friedhoff made a ritual of kissing all the children when he came home. It was peculiar because there never seemed to be any joy in the kissing, neither for Mr. Friedhoff nor for the children. Mr. Friedhoff sat in the big flowered wicker chair by the window, and the children stood in line to be kissed, first Benny, the oldest, then Herb, then Nellilee. Mr. Friedhoff would stare at each of them as they stood in front of him, but there were no kisses in his eyes. He would hold each of them, in turn, firmly by the shoulders and kiss them squarely on the mouth.

Once I was upstairs during the ritual and Mr. Friedhoff tried to kiss me, but I broke away from him.

"You're a little feisty, aren't you?" he said, and he laughed, but it wasn't a pleasant laugh. I was glad I was not a Friedhoff; I was glad I was Mrs. Carrie Hutton Elsea's daughter. Mother was too busy sewing for us, or cooking, or working in the library to have a kissing hour every night, but when she sat up until twelve o'clock to finish a dress for one of us to wear to a party the next day, we knew that was a kiss. Or when we came in from playing at night and found she had made us vegetable soup and our favorite pudding, although she must have been too tired from working at the library all day to move a finger, that was a sort of kiss, too.

"What's that you've got on your lip?" Mr. Friedhoff asked Nellilee when he saw her fever blister.

"It's a fever blister. I've been putting camphor on it all day," Mrs. Friedhoff answered.

Mr. Friedhoff lifted the little girl aside. "I'm not going to kiss a thing like that," he said.

Nellilee put her hand up to her mouth to feel the blister.

"Take your hand down," Mr. Friedhoff said irritably. "Don't touch that thing."

Mrs. Friedhoff kissed Nellilee then, kissed her

two or three times, and smiled at her. "Let's get supper, Nellilee," she said.

Nellilee could not resist touching her lip. She did not do it to be contrary, of that I am sure, but unconsciously her little hand was forever reaching up to feel or scratch at the fever blister.

"That's a pretty bad-looking thing," Mother observed to Mrs. Friedhoff a few days later when she and Nellilee came downstairs to borrow the carpet sweeper.

Mrs. Friedhoff looked worried.

"I know," she said. "If I could only keep Nellilee from scratching at it I think it would get all right. She doesn't mean to, only it bothers her. She's too little to realize it's dangerous to scratch her lip, she'll get it infected."

The blister was a big, brownish-colored scab, distorting the little girl's lip. Nellilee did not stand in line now with her brothers to be kissed in the evenings, but stood over by her mother. After Mr. Friedhoff had kissed Benny and Herb one night, he looked over at Nellilee, whose hand was scratching the blister.

"Stop that," he shouted at her. "I'm not going to tell you again to leave that thing alone."

"Daddy's right, Nellilee," Mrs. Friedhoff said softly. "Please don't touch it. Try to remember."

But Nellilee could not remember. Five minutes later she was touching the scab. Mrs. Friedhoff jerked her hand down, but it was too late. Mr.

Friedhoff had seen her, and he pulled Nellilee over to him roughly and began to whip her.

"Oh, Harry, she's so little," Mrs. Friedhoff cried out.

Nellilee whimpered softly, but she did not cry loudly like the little boys did when their father punished them. That seemed to make Mr. Friedhoff angrier than ever, and he hit her fiercely. Mrs. Friedhoff cried then, a little whimper like Nellilee's.

Nellilee's face was red and hot that evening. The Friedhoffs sat out on the front porch with us for a while after supper, and Mrs. Friedhoff kept feeling Nellilee's forehead. She went upstairs early and put Nellilee to bed and did not come downstairs again. Mr. Friedhoff tried to get Laddie to play with him, but Laddie would not do anything but sit up, again and again, as if he thought that would appease his tormentor and make him go away.

The next day Mrs. Friedhoff had the doctor for Nellilee, and Mother took soup and orange juice upstairs. Nellilee lay in her little baby bed, but the following day the doctor had her moved to the big brass bed, and Mother let the little boys sleep downstairs in our living room. Then came the day I was cautioned not to go upstairs. There was a great bustle in the house, neighbors coming in and out, talking in hushed whispers, bringing offerings of food. Nellilee's baby fingers would never again trouble her lip. They were cold and quiet and dead.

The Friedhoffs did not stay long at our house

after that. The upstairs was very quiet the rest of the time they were there, however; even the boys did not make much noise. Mother brought armloads of romances to Mrs. Friedhoff from the library and did not bother her about them even if they became overdue, but she had no idea if Mrs. Friedhoff ever looked at them.

"I don't believe she ever says a word to him," I heard Mother telling Mrs. Nevins one morning. "She works like she always did, has his meals for him and keeps Benny and Herb clean, but she never speaks to him."

One night she spoke to him, though, a tortured, agonized sentence shattering the quiet. One sentence like the tag end of a thought, words that must have been driving her mad locked up inside of her. I do not know whether Mr. Friedhoff had goaded her to speak or not. The upstairs was still; the little boys must have been put to bed. We had just gone to bed, too, Mother and Helen and Eloise and I. All of a sudden, out of the darkness and quiet, we heard her voice, shrill and almost unrecognizable.

"She was so little, so little!" And then a whimpering sound.

That was what she had said the day Mr. Friedhoff had whipped Nellilee for touching her lip. We listened, waiting for more to be said, but there was no sound. After a while Mr. Friedhoff came down the stairs and went out of the house. Helen said she heard him come in early in the morning.

One other time I heard her speak to him, too. She did talk to him, for all Mother had told Mrs. Nevins, but they were only unimportant words, such as "Harry, supper's ready," or "The paper's here now." It was talk such as might have been said to anyone, it was not as though she were really speaking to him at all. Only this other time, right before they left our house, did it seem as though she was truly speaking to him.

I had been playing with Herb and Benny in their bedroom, and when I came out and started down the stairs I saw Mr. and Mrs. Friedhoff in their living room. Mrs. Friedhoff was sitting on the studio couch sewing, and Mr. Friedhoff, who had been reading the paper, got up suddenly and came over beside her, put his hands on her shoulders, and ran them up and down her arms caressingly.

Mrs. Friedhoff was still for a moment, watching his hands as they moved along the whiteness of her arms. Then she looked at him as she had looked the day I had seen them together by Nellilee's bed, with death around them, that same look of hate and loathing.

"Oh, God, your hands, Harry, your hands," and she tried to push them from her, but he only clamped them tighter about her, while she shut her eyes. Now I knew, I knew, this was the woman of great sorrow; I knew what it meant now. He drew his hands away from her after a moment and laughed, a queer, harsh, triumphant laugh, but she sat there, her eyes shut.

I remember the day the Friedhoffs left our house, and Laddie never forgot it. Mrs. Friedhoff and the two boys were out in front in the car, which was piled with suitcases and boxes. Helen had made Mrs. Friedhoff a box of fudge, and Mother had given her a handmade handkerchief. She had even bought her a new romance to provide her with a happy, make-believe ending, and to help her pretend she had a valiant hero to guard and cherish her in the uncertain years ahead. Mother and Mrs. Friedhoff both cried.

"I don't know where Harry could be," Mrs. Friedhoff said, after she and Benny and Herb had sat out in front in the car for several minutes.

"He went around in back," I said, jumping up on the fender of the car. "I saw him go around there when he came out of the house." And then I remembered that Laddie was there, too; he was sitting on the back porch the last time I had seen him. I ran away from the car, across the yard and around the house, and I saw Mr. Friedhoff.

He was standing on the porch smiling triumphantly as he stared at Laddie, who was sitting up before him, his little back straight and stiff, knowing himself conquered and hating his conqueror. I must have stood there, dazed, a couple of minutes, looking at them both, before I said anything or before they noticed me. How long Laddie had been sitting up I have no idea, but it was surely a record for dog sitters, because when I ran up on the porch Laddie dropped exhausted into my arms. Mr. Friedhoff only laughed, in that same harsh, triumphant way he had laughed at Mrs. Friedhoff, and he went around to the front of the house where his family was waiting for him.

I held Laddie in my arms for a long time, calling him pet names, "nice doggie, little darling, pretty Laddie, brave boy," and stroking his head gently until the shame and hate had gone from his eyes.

I am not today a reader of romances. Mother's — and Montaigne's — abhorrence of such light reading has marked me for life. I was also marked in some way, however, by Mrs. Friedhoff, because I love reading the advertising of such books, and admire their book jackets. I am particularly drawn to the covers of those paperback books called Gothic romances, which usually feature pictures of castles, and beautiful, long-haired maidens in romantic, flowing dresses and billowing capes, running from some dreadful peril.

The maiden in my mind is always Mrs. Friedhoff. The villain, Mr. Friedhoff, who has been pursuing her, has stumbled and fallen into a dark, bottomless lake. But up on the battlements of the castle the hero is looking down at Mrs. Friedhoff and getting ready to rush to her deliverance, and declare his undying love.

THE CONNOISSEUR

Miss Hilda Buck had begun going to funerals regularly because she was disappointed in the library. She had been an almost daily visitor to the library for many years, and had she found there what she was seeking, she would never have turned to what seemed to many persons such a ghoulish pleasure.

Miss Buck lived a few blocks away from us in "the old Buck place," a huge, castlelike house with turrets and fancy trimming around the porch, and stained-glass windows. It was beginning to fall to pieces now after the death of her papa—"she probably hasn't enough income except to eat and sleep on," Mother said—but once the old Buck place had been grand, and the Bucks were a fine old family. So we were proud to be friends of Miss Hilda Buck, even if she was queer about funerals.

Miss Buck was a true connoisseur of funerals. They were her hobby—little ones, big ones, home ones, church ones, even grave services.

"It's a queer interest," Mother admitted to Grandmother, a bit puzzled, "but it's respectable. I don't believe she's thinking of all those people being dead, anyhow. Why, she doesn't even read mysteries."

"Well, it's not as though any of them were murdered," observed Grandmother, who did read mysteries and was addicted to E. Phillips Oppenheim. "They just plain died — I guess," she added, a bit uneasily.

There was no doubt that Miss Buck was respectable. An old maid, everyone called her, although Miss Buck referred to herself, somewhat coyly, as a bachelor girl. When she did this she would always add, rather haughtily, "of my own choice."

I had heard Miss Buck talk to Mother in great detail of the groceryman in Piggly Wiggly's who was a widower with two children and who was always extra nice to her when she came to the store. "Only I don't encourage him," Miss Buck said hastily. As she talked to Mother at the library desk, she always kept peering into the periodical room, or back into the stacks, in hopes that some new man had wandered into the library, a scholar, and lonely.

Once, before her papa died, there had been a magazine salesman who came around every so often, and at one time he had even gone so far as to ask her what she did evenings, but Papa had heard him and had shouted him off the place.

"A magazine salesman," he had puffed, "a magazine salesman for *my* daughter!"

I could always see this romantic picture in my mind when Miss Buck told Mother and me about it, a big stern Papa standing on the front porch and shouting scornfully, "A magazine salesman, a magazine salesman!" as the salesman scampered down Williams Street, his magazines falling out of his bag, trailing in the dust as he ran. Miss Buck, I knew, would have been standing at the front window of the big old Buck homestead, staring after him through the curtains, her heart beating with excitement at being the heroine of this scene.

Miss Buck, like Mother, was an admirer of culture. The attentions of the door-to-door salesman and the widower at Piggly Wiggly made her shiver with excitement, but what she was truly searching for was a permanent relationship with a scholar, like her papa.

"With all those books," she said wistfully to Mother, "you would think the library would be *filled* with scholars."

Mostly, however, it was filled with schoolchildren writing themes, clubwomen hunting material for programs, and casual readers just wanting a book, any book. True, there were the few male regulars, but they buried themselves determinedly in their newspapers or favorite magazines and made it clear to Miss Buck that they had no intentions of becoming involved in a romance.

Everyone had been so kind to Miss Buck when her papa died—"It was such a wonderful funeral!"—that she had then and there developed her present interest in the last rites of others. She had had her glorious hour as her papa's only survivor, with friends and neighbors running in to comfort her and bring her cakes and baked chickens and ham to keep her going. Then came all the pageantry of the lying-in-state at the funeral home, followed by the main event itself, the funeral, in the flower-decked church of which Papa had been, in his day, a pillar. She, Miss Buck, had been the heroine, as Papa was the hero, of it all. It had been a tremendous experience for Miss Buck, and although she still visited the library with some regularity—one never knew when a serious older student of literature might just chance to drop by—she admitted quite honestly to Mother that you met more men at funerals. Why, people had come to Papa's funeral whom she had never seen or even heard of before. Not all of them were scholars, of course, but still and all . . . .

We always knew, when we saw Miss Buck come into the library in her mourning clothes, that she was on her way to a funeral. The sedate, black crepe dress she wore for such occasions was shiny and full of pinpricks at the neck where she fastened on a tiny white lace collar. Her hat was black straw, and she had a bunch of red celluloid cherries that she attached to it when she went to more festive places. Mostly, however, it was plain and unadorned by color. It was her funeral hat.

I had never been to a funeral—I had been only four when my father died and thus too young to be exposed to such sorrow—but I could tell, by the way Miss Buck talked about them, that they were splendid affairs. I had seen funeral processions, the long lines of cars, and the huge hearse that made everyone stop to let it go by. I had stood outside of the Methodist Church and had seen people go in and come away from the funeral. But never, never, had I actually been to one. I did not want to go to a lot of them, like Miss Buck, only to one, and I kept hoping she would ask me to go with her sometime. Usually, though, she went with her cousin Luella.

"Luella does so enjoy a good funeral, too," Miss Buck told Mother. "Only the trouble with Luella," and Miss Buck hesitated, "although of course I wouldn't want you to mention it, is that Luella only goes to the big funerals."

Miss Buck mulled this fact over in her mind for a moment and then went on, troubled. "Now I, Mrs. Elsea, consider it my duty to go to all the funerals open to the public. Supposing everyone thought like Luella does, about not going to funerals of less important persons. There aren't any less important persons after death. Why, even God Himself said that getting a rich man into Heaven was like getting a camel through a needle's eye. Or something like that. That isn't exactly the way God said it," Miss Buck finished, a little confused.

"But it was on that order," said Mother helpfully.
"Yes, that was the idea of it."

Mother bowed before the unquestioned logic of
Miss Buck's statement. It was a good thing, really,
that there were people in the world like Miss Buck,
willing to take the responsibility of going to funerals, even if, on the side, she was hopeful of
striking up an acquaintance with a scholar and
possible suitor. You didn't have any trouble getting
people to go to movies, or to a carnival when it came
to town in summertime, or even to an illustrated
lecture, if it was free. But the average person didn't
just up and go to a funeral.

My hour arrived one summer morning when I was
visiting Miss Buck and helping her shell peas out
on her front porch. I loved going over to Miss Buck's
house, because it was the nearest thing to a castle
I had ever seen, even if it was crumbling. It had
two parlors, a wonderful little cupola room, where
she did her sewing, and a dark, rambling cellar
where some of her papa's favorite bottles of wine
still rested on their sides, covered with cobwebs.
Her papa, Mother said, had been a real terror in his
younger days, even though he was a scholar.

"It's a shame Luella's out of town today," Miss
Buck said, opening up a pod and slipping peas
noisily into the pan. I would use some of the pods
later on in the day for boats to sail in the Nevinses'
rain barrel. "Mrs. Ashley Burns's funeral is this
afternoon. Everyone will be there."

Everyone. Immediately I could see all the residents of Moberly sitting in the Methodist Church, everyone but me.

"I don't see why she had to go out of town this week, of all weeks," Miss Buck went on. "Sometimes it's lonely going to a funeral all by yourself."

"Let me go, too," I said eagerly. "Why can't I go?"

Miss Buck looked at me reflectively.

"Why not?" she asked finally. "Young people have to learn about life sometime."

To learn about death would probably have been a more appropriate statement, but I was too excited at the moment to consider that.

It had not occurred to me that I would meet opposition from Mother.

"Whatever is Miss Buck thinking of?" Mother said, disgustedly. "Funerals aren't for children your age."

"Practically everyone in the world has been but me," I argued quickly. "All my friends have been to one. I never get to see anything but a hearse."

At last, after much discussion with Grandmother, Mother agreed to let me go. "Only I'll have to get out the iron right this minute and iron your apple dress."

My apple dress was my good summer dress. It was pale blue, with a red apple appliqued on each pocket, and I wore it each Sunday to Sunday School. I realized despairingly that I couldn't go to the funeral after all. I couldn't go in my apple dress. I had to wear black, black was essential. I remembered Miss Buck telling me with horror of Mr. Latimer, who had worn a gray suit striped in red while he was lying in his coffin, and recalled hearing Miss Buck *tck tck* softly to herself, saying his family should have known better than to dress him in that. Everyone knew that a gray suit, especially striped in red, was no kind in which to meet one's Maker.

"He had a red-colored wart on his chin that just matched that stripe," Miss Buck had said, reminiscently. "And there was a hair sticking out of the very middle of that wart. You would have thought they'd have pulled it."

It was as important for people who attended funerals to be dressed correctly as it was for the corpse. I could imagine Miss Buck's horror at seeing me ready to accompany her to the funeral this afternoon, wearing a dress with apples on the pockets, she in her correct black silk and her plain black hat with the cherries taken off of it.

"I can't go," I cried hopelessly. "I can't wear my apple dress. I've got to have a black dress, and I don't have."

"That's nonsense," Mother replied matter-of-factly. "A child doesn't have to wear black. You'll look clean and neat in your apple dress and that's all that matters."

All at once I knew that I *could* go to the funeral, after all. "Dark blue and black," I had heard Miss

Buck say, "are the only decent colors for the deceased to wear." And if it was correct for the deceased to wear dark blue, then surely it would be all right for me. I had a dark blue dress, a winter wool serge.

"Where's my blue serge I wore last winter? I'll have to wear that," I shouted, hopping excitedly about the room.

"It's wrapped up with moth balls and in the closet for next winter." Mother was beginning to lose her patience. "You'll burn up wearing wool in the middle of July."

But I was not to be kept from attending this funeral or attending it correctly attired. Everybody would be there, Miss Buck had said so. And they would not see me in an apple dress but in approved dark blue.

Miss Buck and I left for the funeral with a half hour to our credit, since the Methodist Church was just three blocks away. I was almost smothering in my winter serge, but I had looked in the mirror and had approved of what I saw.

"You smell like moth balls," Eloise snickered.

"When she gets in the sun she'll air out," Mother said, folding up the brown paper that was marked "Peg's blue winter serge." "Besides, there are always so many flowers in the church no one will even notice moth ball smell."

"It's a fine day for a funeral," Miss Buck said approvingly, as we walked down Fourth Street. Oh, it was a wonderful day, the day of days. I was at last going to a funeral with Miss Buck.

"I had intended to go to the Burnses' home before the service," Miss Buck said confidentially, "but I was afraid we might be late to the church. And besides I was over there last night and saw all the flowers and Mrs. Burns."

I said nothing. I was too blissfully happy. Not for me today to talk, merely to exist, to accept.

"Mrs. Burns didn't look a bit like herself," Miss Buck was saying. "They'd gotten a hairdresser to curl her hair a bit and it changed her whole appearance. Sarah Burns has always had straight hair and would never even put it up on curlers or pins, because she thought it was the Lord's will if she had straight hair, and she had no business to frizz it up."

Miss Buck did not think the Lord minded if you tried to curl your hair, I knew. I had seen her once early in the morning, her straight brown hair twisted about dozens of curlers, until she was a strange Medusa, her head writhing with little leather snakes.

"A funeral really takes up most of your day," Miss Buck sighed contentedly as we neared the church, "if one goes to the home before the service and then to the service proper, and then to the cemetery for the burying after the church ceremony."

"We're getting here early," she whispered, as we walked in the church. "We'll get to watch all the people come in."

Miss Buck chose a pew far down the aisle. She had told me she could never decide whether it was best to sit close up in front so she would not miss a bit of the service, not an *Amen* from the preacher, nor a sniffle from the relatives, or whether it was preferable to place one's self at the back where one didn't have to crane one's neck to see everyone who came in.

Not many people were there when we arrived, and I was disappointed, having expected to see everybody, even the Mayor and the Boy Scouts, as at the band concerts in the park. The flowers were being brought in as we came, however, and were being banked in the front. There were carnations and lilies and roses and elaborate artificial wreaths of silvered leaves tied with lavender and pink tulle bows.

"That's mine," Miss Buck whispered, nodding toward a conservative wreath of little white flowers and lots of greenery. "It shows up right well, I think," and she looked proud. "I never order by phone, like some people do; I pick them out myself. And of course I don't send flowers to everybody. I really couldn't afford that."

Now Mrs. Hickock began to play softly on the church organ, a sad, somber piece, and all of a sudden the church was crowded. The pallbearers padded softly down the aisle on either side of the coffin and sat down in back of the family.

"Not shedding a tear," Miss Buck whispered

suddenly, looking over toward Mr. Burns accusingly. Mr. Burns was sitting up very straight, looking directly in front of him, and he was surrounded by a group of weeping relatives, but he was not crying.

Everything was very quiet. The music had stopped, and nothing at all could be heard but a few subdued snifflings from down in front where the family sat. The preacher had his Bible before him and was beginning the service. Reverend Black was praising Mrs. Burns now, calling her a beloved mother and wife. Mr. Burns still wasn't crying.

"Mrs. Burns would be furious if she knew," Miss Buck whispered, outraged. She was trembling, and her fingers fumbled awkwardly with her handkerchief. She wept softly at first, then she pressed the wet ball of her handkerchief to her eyes and her shoulders shook with hiccuping sobs.

"Furious," I heard her hiss out again between hiccups.

I stared at Mr. Burns curiously. He was sitting stiffly in the family pew, staring straight ahead still, like a solid unmoved rock among the waves of audible mourning splashing around him.

"They don't get along," I had heard people say about Mr. and Mrs. Burns. But even so, it would be nice if he'd cry about her, especially when everybody else was. I even began to cry. Suddenly I was miserable. I was smothering in my serge, and it was scratching me. In winter I had a layer of long underwear under it as a buffer between it and my skin, but my scant summer bloomers and thin petticoat were no protection. And the moth ball smell had not aired out in the sun, as Mother said it would. It floated pungently around the pew, mortifying, insidious, not to be covered up with lily and carnation perfume from the wreaths. I burned, I itched, I was odorous. And I remembered that I had forgotten to save any pea pods to sail in the rain barrel.

At last the funeral was over, and Miss Buck and I followed the casket and the crowd out of the church. Miss Buck was still weeping, harder, it seemed to me, than anyone, and I began to grow embarrassed. People were looking at her solicitously, and one woman even put her arm about her kindly and whispered, "Poor dear Miss Hilda, I didn't know you had been so close to her." But this only sent Miss Buck into another shivering spasm of weeping and blowing her nose.

People were piling into cars to go out to the cemetery, and Miss Buck teetered uncertainly in front of the church. Mr. Burns was standing by a car helping his two sisters step into it. He was looking curiously at Miss Buck and had a surprised look on his face, as though saying to himself if she, Miss Buck, not even a relative, had felt so desolate about his wife's death, surely, he, too, should be feeling more.

Then he was beside her, taking a gentle hold on

her arm as she balanced unsteadily on the curbing.

"Won't you ride in our car, Miss Hilda?" he asked. "There's plenty of room if you'd like to go with us."

Miss Buck fairly flew to the automobile, forgetting me completely. After she got into the car she did think about me again and gave a startled, guilty look out of the window, and opened the car door as though to ask me to get in. But I turned away from her quickly and pushed through the funeral crowd. I did not want to go to the cemetery; I did not want to hear Miss Buck crying. When I was halfway down the block I began to skip and to sing under my breath, "Will you *wait* for me *there*," making my voice tremble like Miss Jennie's, who sang at the funeral, "by the *beautiful shore*. . . ."

"I've been to a funeral," I shouted to my friend Jack Nevins when I got home.

Jack looked up from his pea pod boats that were navigating the rain barrel at the back of the house. "You think you're smart, is all," he yelled, shaking the rain barrel to make waves for the boat.

"A *funeral*, a *funeral*," I kept singing, as I yanked off my heavy blue serge, put on a red gingham, and snatched a handful of potato peelings out of the garbage so that I could sail them with Jack.

When Miss Buck and Mr. Burns got married several months later, Mother and the neighbors talked about nothing else for weeks. Imagine, Miss Buck getting married at her age! – although Mother remembered that Mr. Carnegie himself did not marry until his middle life. Certainly funerals had proved, in Miss Buck's case at least, to be more rewarding socially than the library. Mr. Burns might not be exactly the most cultured man in the world, but perhaps it was just as well, when you remembered some of the cultured gentlemen in the library with whom Miss Hilda had tried to strike up acquaintance, and who had kept their eyes severely on their books.

The newlyweds would live in the old Buck place, which Mr. Burns had been heard to say he hoped to restore to its former glory, the way it was when Judge Buck had been in his prime. As to Judge Buck's bottles of wine still resting in the wine cellar, once Ashley Burns moved in there, Mother said, the cobwebs would not be on them much longer, you could count on *that*.

"I thought you didn't like him," I said accusingly to Miss Buck a few days before her wedding.

"Not like Mr. Burns?" Miss Buck was horrified. "Why, how could anyone help liking a good, kind man like Mr. Burns?"

But my memory was long.

"He didn't cry at the funeral," I said. "When Mrs. Burns died he didn't shed a tear."

I thought a shadow passed over Miss Buck's face. Then she laughed gaily. "Why, what a thing to remember," she said archly.

She was very gay these days, Miss Buck, the heroine of a scene more exciting even than that which had centered around the salesman when Papa was alive, or even Papa's funeral. She invited me over to see her wedding presents and her wedding dress, a navy-blue silk — "I couldn't wear white, of course, this soon after Mr. Burns's bereavement" — which I was sure would be her new funeral dress, too, to relieve the wear on the black one she had worn for so long.

"Even though she's finally met her man," I had heard Mother say confidentially to Grandmother, "I think she's got the funeral habit by now and can't give it up."

Miss Buck was all delight and giggles when she showed me the lace tidies she had worked, and rugs she had braided, and her mother's silver. She was still gay when I ran outside to get her mail, but when I came back into the house she was looking thoughtful again.

"What a thing to remember," I heard her say softly, but she was not speaking to me. And she smoothed her new navy wedding-funeral dress carefully and held it closely, almost fiercely, against her.

8

FAREWELL OYSTERS ROCKEFELLER

For one whole glorious week during a summer of the early twenties, the residents of our landlocked Midwestern town journeyed to Europe. That is, all of the residents who took advantage of "Let's Travel Abroad with Cookbooks Week," which Mother organized at the library.

"Let's Go to France with Oxtails Parisienne et Petits Pois à la Française."

"Let's Go to England with Roast Beef and Yorkshire Pudding."

"Let's Go to Germany with Sauerbraten and Kartoffel Klasse." (The latter turned out to be plain old potato dumplings.)

Mother refused, however, to give any advertising to the revolting German dish of hassenpfeffer. She hated the idea of eating rabbits, especially since we had one as a pet. Nor would she play up French beef bourguignon. It may be true, as the cookbooks said, that alcohol evaporated in cooking, but wine for the pot could just as easily be utilized as wine for the table, and thus one was started on the long road from which there is no returning; namely, the road to drunkenness and ruin.

Moberly was probably filled with a great many grouchy men during "Let's Travel Abroad" week. Otherwise stolid housewives were adventurous when it came to their kitchens, but strangely enough, otherwise adventurous men were downright prudes when their eating habits were imperiled. There was nothing wrong with good old American steak and potatoes and hot biscuits and apple pie. None of this Frenchy stuff on the table, for God's sake.

The threat to the sacred masculine steak and potatoes menu was brought about indirectly because of Myrtle Shanks and her discovery of Mr. Carnegie's Lib'ary.

Myrtle was sixteen and her mother (Just Billie Dearie) was thirty-four when they came to live in our apartment. Both of them worked at the shoe factory, the industry that was Moberly's main boast to being a factory town. We had never had "shoe factory folks" as renters before; Mother had specialized in cultured couples and ex-school-teachers and others of a more or less white-collar profession. But the percentage of culture-seeking renters was rather low this spring. Our upstairs had been unoccupied for almost a month, even though it had been advertised as a spacious two-room and kitchenette apartment; later, when that found no takers, one of the rooms and the kitchenette had been offered, also unsuccessfully, as a cozy and cheaper Real Home For Someone.

Myrtle wore mascara and spit curls, dreadful fishhooks of hair flattened against the forehead or cheeks and stiffened with soap to make them lie flat. But in that era Helen and Eloise considered them very fashionable, and to me—I was only nine—anything worn by anyone older than I was fashionable. Eloise was fifteen and Helen was sixteen, but Myrtle seemed years older than either of them. She walked on high, teetering heels, and Mother thought her dresses were too tight and too gaudy. She hung dangling black earrings in her ears and she went with a man who was twenty-six. She was another way of life, she was the Shoe Factory Girl.

Myrtle's mother dressed very much as her daughter did, only her spit curls were bigger and stiffer. She was forever reminding us that she had married when she was only a baby. "No older than Baby here," she would say, pointing to Myrtle.

Her name was Mrs. Harris, but she did not like us to call her that because she and Mr. Harris were separated. "Just call me Billie, dearie," she would remind us, "just Billie, dearie."

Myrtle's name wasn't Harris at all, it was Shanks, and that was confusing until Mrs. Harris explained that Myrtle was the daughter of her first husband,

Jerry Shanks, and that old man Harris had nothing to do with that at all.

"Not a thing," she emphasized, almost belligerently. "He can think what he likes, but Myrtle's a Shanks through and through."

That was logical and easily understood. If Myrtle was Mr. Shanks's daughter, she certainly was not Mr. Harris' child, and there was no reason for Just Billie Dearie to get so excited when she spoke about her second and absent husband.

"That woman has lived," I heard Mrs. Nevins remark sagely to Mother one day, as they watched Just Billie Dearie walk down the street.

Mother didn't like Helen and Eloise and me to visit with Myrtle and her mother, but we found them and their little apartment irresistible. Strange people were always coming in and out, and there was always laughing there and the sound of excitement. We would look out the window at all the visitors who came, and would sometimes purposely lie in our upstairs bedroom and pretend to be asleep in order to listen to what was going on in the next room, where Myrtle and her mother were having company. We learned then that they played poker, they and their guests, and sometimes they drank beer. If Mother had known about the poker and the beer she would have made them move.

"We never had anything in my house or in Papa's house to drink in all of my life," Mother was proud of saying. But if she said this when Grandmother was around, Grandmother would protest.

"Now, Carrie, you know very well Joe liked his bit of wine"—Joe was Grandfather—"and you and Luther had ten quarts of fermented grape juice down in the basement the winter before Peggy was born."

"We didn't know it was fermented," Mother would say defensively.

"But it was and you drank it," Grandmother said triumphantly. It wasn't often anyone could have the last word with Mother, but Grandmother had it now and she knew it.

The excitement surrounding Myrtle and Just Billie Dearie was climaxed one night when Mother went to Eastern Star. Eastern Star meetings were always long ones, and Mother never got home until eleven o'clock or after on those nights. Those were the evenings, when we three girls were alone in the house, that the wind howled the loudest and the floor boards squeaked the noisiest, and one of us always said, "Supposing someone was outside the window right this minute looking in at us."

Eloise had just gotten through saying this about nine o'clock one night when Helen walked bravely to the window, pulled aside the curtain and looked out, gave a little cry, and came running back to where Eloise and I were sitting.

"Someone *is* looking in," she said. "Someone is standing out on the sidewalk this minute, a man!"

The door opening from the downstairs hall into

our part of the house was locked, but the front door, as a rule, was left unfastened until later in the evening, and the last one in locked the door. We crowded together in the middle of the living room, terrified, and heard the front door open slowly and close, and soft footsteps going up the front stairs. Laddie, who should have been barking furiously at this intrusion, was roaming somewhere about the neighborhood, and thus could not protect us.

"Maybe he's going to see Mrs. Harris or Myrtle," Helen whispered, but we all knew that Myrtle and Just Billie Dearie were not at home. Myrtle had gone out with her twenty-six-year-old admirer, and Mrs. Harris had gone out alone not long afterward, although she had met a man down at the corner of Logan and Fourth streets. We could hear footsteps moving around upstairs, but soon they ceased, and there was no sound from above at all.

"Run over to Nevinses', Eloise," Helen said, appearing to be very brave. "Tell Mr. Nevins you're scared and to come over."

Eloise looked at Helen as though she had been told to jump over Niagara Falls barefoot.

"Unlock the door and go out in the dark?" she asked, horrified. "I'd sooner die. He might have come down the stairs and be standing right outside our door this minute." She gave a terrified moan.

"Silly, it's nothing to be scared of, go ahead," Helen urged, but she was trembling.

"Go yourself, you're so brave."

"Mama told me not to leave the house, to look after Peggy."

"If we could only get to the telephone," Eloise whispered.

But that was out of the question. To get to the telephone one of us would have to unlock the door, go into the dark hall, turn on the light — expecting any moment a chill hand on her shoulder, a black form at her back — and then ascend the long, badly lit stairs that led to the telephone, as well as to the darkness and unknown of the rented room.

We had no idea how long we huddled together, terrified, in the living room, aware of every sound in the house. Once the telephone rang, shrill and loud, but we let it ring, although the jangle of it in the stillness only added to our terror. Laddie, who had treacherously let a monster come into the house he was supposed to guard, was whining at the front door to come in, but we did not dare go to his rescue. Finally Helen cautiously lifted up a window and craned her neck to look upstairs.

"It's dark as pitch," she reported, hastily closing and locking the window. "He's up there in the dark, waiting."

We felt a chill of horror and delicious excitement.

"Who do you suppose he's waiting for, Myrtle or Just Billie Dearie?" Eloise whispered.

"For Just Billie Dearie, of course. Myrtle has only one man, but Mrs. Harris has dozens of them. This is one of them."

"What'll he do?" and my legs began to shake. "What's he waiting for her for?"

"I guess she's been untrue," Helen said, looking very wise. "And he's going to wreak his vengeance."

"How does he wreak it?"

"Choke her, maybe. Or if he has a knife he'll cut her throat." Helen had read some of Myrtle's *True Mystery* magazines.

At the end of this frightful sentence we heard footsteps coming slowly down the stairs. Did they stop in front of our door for an instant? We held our breath and each other's hands. The front door opened and closed. We heard Laddie, trying to redeem himself for his earlier carelessness, bark madly, and then a string of terrible curses.

Helen ran to the window. "He's limping down the walk," she called back in a hoarse whisper. "I think Laddie bit him. Now he's going down the street. He's gone, he's gone!"

But still we would not venture outside the door, not even to let Laddie in, although he barked wildly and constantly. He was furious that any intruder had dared to enter our house, and more furious at himself for his defection from duty. For all he knew, his charges were lying inside the house dead at the hands of a fiend. Helen kept her post at the window. Perhaps the man was lurking in the shadows down the street and would creep up again.

"She's coming, here she comes," Helen announced suddenly, and she ran to our door and unlocked it as

Mrs. Harris and Laddie came in the front door. Laddie ran from one of us to the other, leaping against us joyfully, kissing us when he could, whining with delight at finding us alive.

"He just left, a few minutes ago," Eloise cried out to Mrs. Harris.

"He's been hiding upstairs in your room for hours, waiting for you!" Helen wanted to tell about it herself. It was her story, really; it was she who had seen the man on the sidewalk, had seen him come and had seen him go.

After she had heard our stories, Just Billie Dearie turned on the porch light and looked out in the darkness.

"I guess I know who it was, all right," she said, and she tossed her head saucily, her stiffened spit curls flopping against her forehead. "I told Lew Harris I'd find someone to give me these!"—and she pulled from her bosom a necklace of huge imitation pearls and held them triumphantly in front of her. She did not seem to be talking to us, but to the man somewhere out in the darkness, the man who for a couple of terrifying hours this night had been part of the shadows of her room. The pearls shone under the electric light, white and dazzling and, somehow, wicked. We gaped at them, never having seen their like before, except in movies. Pola Negri and Gloria Swanson wore such jewels. There was an ugly look on Mrs. Harris' face as she fingered the pearls. I had always thought she was pretty, but now she appeared rough and frightful, witchlike, her claws of hands clutching the huge pearls as though thrusting them before her for all the world, and especially the man in the shadows, to see.

At this moment Mother arrived home, riding in the same car with the Worthy Matron and two Star Points, and Mrs. Harris hastily thrust the pearls back into the depth and mystery of her bosom. "I'm not afraid of no man," she said as she ran up the stairs, but we noticed that when she got to the top she stopped for a moment and looked behind her as though for reassurance, and then tripped on uncertainly into the darkness of her room.

Mother worried about Myrtle.

"There's no need to," Mrs. Nevins told her. "If her own mother doesn't worry, why should you?"

"That's just it. Somebody's got to worry," Mother insisted. Because to her it was incredible that a child should not be worried about. Helen and Eloise and I were excellent examples showing that worry was essential.

But Myrtle came and went as she pleased, sometimes with her mother and sometimes with Frank, the man who visited her more than any of the others, and sometimes by herself. She was young and silly, and she giggled in a high squeaky voice, but always she seemed older and more the mother than Just Billie Dearie was. When Mrs. Harris fixed supper she usually had cold lunch meat and yesterday's potatoes sliced up unheated and a can of pork and beans. But Myrtle liked to cook and was always making puddings and fixing salads and baking biscuits or cakes.

It troubled Mother to see Myrtle go out with her young man, knowing that Mrs. Harris never bothered to ask her where she was going and who she would be with and to tell her to be sure to be home not later than eleven o'clock. I think she would have taken it upon herself to ask Myrtle these things, if Myrtle did not seem so wise and all-knowing. Eloise and Helen at fifteen and sixteen were still children. Myrtle had passed them years ago. It seemed possible she had never really been a child.

Myrtle had never been in a library before she moved to our house, and it was not love of literature that finally brought her there but love of cooking and homemaking. Helen had brought a cookbook home from the library and Myrtle read it through from cover to cover. She would even come running downstairs to repeat a fancy recipe to us, or have us taste some marvel she had made, one-egg fudge loaf, steamed apple suet pudding, chicken terrapin, canned veal mousse, or shrimp wiggle. It frustrated her, however, when she did not know the meaning of some of the words she encountered, such as *shallots, fines herbes, chiffonade, fumet, crepes.*

One cookbook was only an appetizer to Myrtle. When she heard there were many different kinds of cookbooks in the library, she could not wait to come visit such a wonderful place. Mother recognized the importance of catering to people's stomachs as well as their minds, and besides *she* liked to cook. But it was Myrtle's excitement over the cookbook section that inspired Mother to have the "Let's Travel Abroad with Cookbooks Week" at the library.

Myrtle read the cookbooks as though they were novels. Oysters Rockefeller and beef Wellington produced in her the same emotional thrill that readers of fine literature experienced. I think I was still immersed in Dorothy Dainty and the Little Colonel books in those days, so my emotional thrills were possibly at a lower level than Myrtle's. Myrtle also ventured timidly into the periodical room and fingered the homemaking magazines lovingly. There was not too much she could do to rearrange our simple little furnished apartment, but she pushed furniture about, added a little rickrack trim to the kitchen curtains, and made a cross-stitch cushion for the studio couch. She even asked if she could cut a few roses to arrange as a table centerpiece. Mother, who longed for everyone to better himself, had dreams that Myrtle would rise above her background. Cookbooks were well and good, there was nothing wrong with creative homemaking, but if Myrtle could also become interested in good literature, she might even go back to high school, even — ah, what a dreamer my mother was! — go to college like her own daughters would do. Myrtle might be a home economist!

Summer nights were the best nights. In the long summer evenings everyone sat on front porches drinking lemonade or iced tea and called across yards to each other, and Jack Nevins and I caught lightning bugs and put them in jars for torches. Jack and I were sitting on the front porch steps with our lightning bugs one night just after dusk when Myrtle and Frank came up the walk, very gay and excited.

"You're awfully dressed up for your date tonight, Myrtle," I said, admiring her beautiful white dress. It was a new one, very tight, like all of her dresses, and with a lot of ruffles at the neck. She was wearing flowers at her shoulder, flimsy little sweet peas clustered about a rose.

They both laughed.

"D'ye hear that, Myrtle? All dressed up for your big date." Frank took hold of her arm, which jingled with bracelets, and put it through his.

"Oh, you silly," Myrtle said to him, and she laughed harder than ever. They went on in the house and up the stairs.

Long after Jack and I had played with the lightning bugs and let them fly away again, I saw Mother and Grandmother huddled together on the front porch talking in whispers. Every once in a while one of them would go out in the yard and look upstairs.

"It's completely dark up there, Mama," I heard

Mother say. "Not a sign of a light. And I'm sure they never came downstairs after they went up this evening."

"Where's her mother, for land's sake," Grandmother muttered. "What's her mother thinking of?"

"A sixteen-year-old girl and a man ten years older than she is, what can you expect?" Mother asked of no one in particular, as though she herself were trying to solve the problem.

Mrs. Nevins walked across the yard and sat down in the swing by Mother.

"Jim wants to know if everything's all right," Mrs. Nevins said anxiously. "He says you've been looking up as though you thought the roof might be on fire."

Mother gave a little gasp. "It wasn't anything," she said, but her voice sounded strained. "Tell Mr. Nevins not to give it a thought. Mama thought she heard squirrels on the roof."

"Squirrels on the roof," Mrs. Nevins said thoughtfully.

"Why, Carrie!" Grandmother protested.

"But it's all right," Mother said. "I'm sure there aren't any."

There was a little silence.

"Your roomers aren't much company, are they?" Mrs. Nevins asked, after a moment or so. "Always off away somewhere."

"When they aren't home it's just all the quieter," Mother said. "We hardly know we've got roomers, really. That's the way we like it to be."

"I thought I saw Myrtle and her beau come in tonight," Mrs. Nevins said pleasantly. "She was all dressed up fit to kill."

"I didn't notice," Mother answered.

"It's the funniest thing. I was telling Jim, I saw them come in but I never did see them leave again, only they must have; the upstairs is all dark."

"They probably went to a picture show. Gloria Swanson's at the Grand."

"Oh. . . ."

There was another silence.

"I hate to tell you this, Mrs. Elsea, but I think they're still upstairs. I don't think they ever did go out after they came in. And the lights went out an hour ago, if not longer."

Mother gave a cry of dismay.

"I didn't know it had been that long," she whispered.

"Every bit of it."

"I've been almost crazy," and Mother sounded as though she was glad, after all, to confide in her neighbor. "I've been saying to Mama, shall I go upstairs and make them turn on the light, or shall I wait until her mother comes home and let her tend to it? And all the time, they're up there, the light's out, and the whole neighborhood wondering, I guess."

"Maybe Jim could tend to it," Mrs. Nevins said helpfully. "Shall I have him come over?"

"Oh, no, no." Suddenly Mother stiffened. "There's Mrs. Harris," she whispered. "There she comes down the street."

Mother got up from the swing and went to the edge of the porch, Grandmother and Mrs. Nevins following her. But it did not look as though Mrs. Harris were going to come home after all. She passed by our walk and was almost to the alley when Mother called out to her, sharply, and with panic in her voice.

"Why, hello," Just Billie Dearie said pleasantly. "Looks like you all are having a party up on the porch." Then, as an afterthought, "Myrtle and Frank home yet?"

"They're up there," Mother answered, her voice cold and stony. "But you'd never know it. Not a light on in the place."

"Bless their hearts," Mrs. Harris said. "Bless their little hearts."

"Bless their—" Mother suddenly found herself tongue-tied.

"I'm staying at my sister's down the street tonight," Mrs. Harris went on. "I forgot my nightgown, but of course I wouldn't disturb Myrtle and Frank for worlds. I'll make Mettie lend me one of hers."

"You're not going to disturb them?" Mother's voice was shrill and full of horror.

"You're only married once," Mrs. Harris giggled. "That is, you should be. I don't count. I didn't mean to be married twice." And she teetered off down the street to sister Mettie's, calling back that the marriage was a secret, not to let on to a soul.

Mother sank down on the swing. "Married," she said, and she looked curiously toward the dark, second-story window.

"Just Helen's age," Grandmother said. And she looked upstairs, too.

I got up from the steps and ran onto the porch. "Why aren't they having a party?" I asked, disappointed. "If Myrtle and Frank just got married why don't they have a party tonight and have punch?"

But no one answered me. Mother, for all she was a dreamer, knew that Myrtle would never go on to good literature. In all probability she would even forget about oysters Rockefeller and beef bourguignon.

9

STORK SHOWER

Leda Maude Wilson did not have her baby in the children's room of the library, although this was a fearful possibility that haunted Mother all during Leda Maude's visit to her mother when I was ten years old.

Leda Maude came into the library regularly at nine o'clock every morning during those spring weeks she spent back home with her mother before her baby was born. Home was our apartment, where her mother had lived ever since Leda Maude had gone to St. Louis to work, several months before. During the morning Leda Maude moved from room to room of the library. First, she read the daily papers, the *St. Louis Post Dispatch*, since St. Louis was where her husband worked, and then the *Moberly Monitor-Index*, and sometimes even the *Chicago Tribune*, although she knew no one in Chicago. After that, she paced restlessly about in the periodical section, selecting magazine after magazine, thumbing quickly through each one as though it were a duty instead of a pleasure. By that time, most of the morning was gone, and she walked slowly home to have dinner—which most Moberly folk in those days had at noon—with her mother.

Mother wasn't quite sure that she wanted Leda Maude Wilson to visit in our upstairs apartment in her Condition.

"If it wasn't for the fact that her mother already lives there and wants Leda Maude for company, I'd never have said it would be all right for her to come," she asserted grimly to Grandmother. "I'd rather the girls didn't run up against anything like that until they're older. And at a time like this," she added, "a woman shouldn't be wasting her days and nights in a *library*." This sounded strange coming from Mother, who usually advised a good book as a cure for any sorrow or snag that life presented.

At first I had no idea what Leda Maude's Condition was. It was something mysterious and unmentionable, indicated by low whispers and significant looks between the neighbors. There was nothing strange-looking about Leda Maude to me. Her stomach stuck out in front like a bundle under her dress, but otherwise she was so pretty that you forgot her funny stomach and never thought about calling her Fatty.

It was my best friend Annabel who told me what

Leda Maude's Condition was.

"She's going to have a baby," she whispered one day when Leda Maude came out of the house and walked down the street.

"How do you know?" I asked curiously. Annabel always seemed to know things I did not. She was a source of infinite wisdom, generous with her knowledge, but sometimes superciliously explanatory.

"Her stomach," Annabel went on in a whisper. "See how her stomach sticks out?"

"Yes."

"Well, that's where the baby is."

I looked at her in amazement. "How does it get *there*?" The whole thing was incredible.

Annabel herself wasn't quite sure about this. "Frances says it comes because of love. You love someone and the baby comes."

After this, Leda Maude seemed more interesting to me than ever, with a whole baby inside of her stomach. That lump in the front of her dress was the baby, and all because she loved someone.

Leda Maude was quiet and did not go out much, except to the library every morning and on solitary walks in the early evening, usually ending up at the library. In her evening library visits she spent most of her time in the children's room, going through the books for the very youngest, as though preparing already for her role as a parent. Mother was glad most of the children did not come to the library later in the evening, since Leda Maude made such a habit of it, and her Condition was so obvious.

"Now, I'm no prude, Mama," she told Grandmother, "but the Lord knows I don't want her to go into labor in the children's room, of all places. Even if children aren't around—and God forbid they would be."

One evening I saw Leda Maude out in the garden all by herself, her hand gently stroking the leaves of the lilac bush, which was filled with tiny, grapelike buds. She touched the buds softly and put her face close to them.

"I have come back," I heard her whisper, and she seemed to be crying. "Oh, be glad, be glad, be close to me, lilac," and she had broken off one of the tiny branches before she went into the house. I hoped no one else had seen her. I didn't know why, only I felt it was all right for me to have seen her and heard her, but not anyone else.

"She's really not more than a baby herself," Leda Maude's mother told Mother one day. I saw her look out of the window into the yard where Leda Maude was sitting in the swing, her head leaning against the back of the swing and her eyes shut. Her hands were clasped in her lap under the baby and her hair tumbled over her forehead.

"It's so strange to think of little Leda Maude having a husband and going to have a baby," she went on, not noticing Mother's quick disapproving look in my direction.

"I'm glad he has money," Mrs. Mainwaring said happily, "so Leda Maude will never have to go without. And I'm glad he's handsome, like Leda Maude's husband should be."

Leda Maude had a picture of Alfred — his full name was Alfred Forrest Wilson — in a large black and gilt frame on her dresser. He was very blonde and handsome, and he had written in a beautiful, spidery handwriting down at the bottom, "Always, Alfred."

"Leda Maude's done well," Mrs. Mainwaring continued, "better than any of the other girls her age, even though for a while I was worried she might be an old maid, with all her talk about wanting a career before she got married."

Mother sniffed, ever so slightly, so possibly Mrs. Mainwaring did not hear her, but I was well acquainted with Mother's sniffs, and knew, from what I had heard her tell the neighbors, that she thought Leda Maude was far too young to have gotten married. With Mother, a girl's education, not her marriage, was the important thing. Her girls would go through college and be schoolteachers. Marriage could always come later.

Mrs. Mainwaring was happily unaware of Mother's disapproval.

"Jim Wheeler was dead set on her before she went away to work in St. Louis," Mrs. Mainwaring was chattering. "Leda Maude was always nice to him, but she wanted that career and never could make up her mind about him. So finally, a little while after she left, that's when he married Donna Jones. But even so, you should have seen him stare at her the other day downtown, like he couldn't get his fill of her."

I knew that myself—that Jim Wheeler still stared at her, I mean. He had been in the library one night when Leda Maude was there, and he tried to talk to her, following her about from one area of shelves to another. Once I heard him say, "Leda Maude, you should never have gone away. What was I to think?" But Leda Maude, who was usually very gentle and kind, would not even speak to him. He kept looking around nervously as though he expected someone to be watching them, but, as Mother already observed, no one was usually in the children's room this late in the evening—only me, when I came down to walk home with Mother. Even that was only when I had nothing more exciting to do.

Jim kept following Leda Maude around the room and trying to talk to her, until finally Leda Maude did say something. She stood very straight and still in front of him and spoke.

"The library rules say 'quiet,' Jim. You don't want Mrs. Elsea coming in here and hearing you—or Donna."

There was no expression on her face at all as she spoke, but Jim looked as though he were going to cry—a grown man almost crying right there in public in the library. Then he said hopelessly, "Oh, my God," and turned and walked away from Leda Maude and out of the library.

Leda Maude's mother would not have liked Jim Wheeler bothering Leda Maude.

"I'm glad Leda Maude didn't take Jim," she had said to Mother the day she told her about Jim's being dead set on Leda Maude last year. "I always hoped she'd marry someone wonderful and romantic, not a boy she'd known all her life. Why, she never looked at another boy but Jim all through high school. I can hardly wait to meet Alfred. He's in the publishing business, you know, and goodness knows when he'll get to come here for a visit, he's so busy. He'll not want Leda Maude out of his sight for long, so I'm enjoying every minute she's here."

I could tell Alfred was wonderful by the way he looked out of that elegant frame, sort of nonchalant and gay, and by the way his hair was brushed back until every wave seemed to have been carved with a very fine comb. The boys I knew did not look like that, not Egg Carter, nor Billy, nor Joseph, nor anybody else in town. I knew why Leda Maude loved him. I would have adored him, too. Oh, wonderful St. Louis Alfred, lover of Leda Maude!

One Saturday afternoon Leda Maude and her mother were downstairs in our living room, which Mother had told Mrs. Mainwaring she could use for a surprise stork shower for Leda Maude. I could hear all three of them talking, Mother and Mrs. Mainwaring casually, so Leda Maude would not suspect anything. It was not yet time for the guests to arrive, and I had been asked by Mrs. Mainwaring to run up to her apartment and bring her glasses down to her. After picking up the glasses in the little parlor, I could see beyond into the bedroom, where Alfred's picture stood prominently on the dresser. As I stared through the doorway I became bolder, and cautiously, softly, edged myself into the bedroom. Leda Maude had all sorts of cosmetics that Helen and Eloise and I longed to have. Helen had some face creams, too, because she was almost Leda Maude's age, but they were not wonderful like this. Oh, to meet someone like Alfred when I grew up! Not that I was still a little girl anymore, though, and if Mother would let me use creams and things like Leda Maude used, I'd look almost as old.

Forgetful of the danger of being, uninvited, in the bedroom by myself, I threw my hair carelessly over my forehead like Leda Maude wore hers, and leaned my elbows on the dressing table. I looked intently into the mirror, pretending I saw no freckles, and then turned toward Alfred.

"I'm Peggy, Alfred," I whispered. "Am I almost as beautiful, am I, see, with my hair fluffed out like Leda Maude's?"

"Very beautiful," the elegant Alfred smiled, becoming very alive in his frame. "And you look every bit as old as Leda Maude does. I shouldn't wonder there weren't a lot of young men who think you're mighty nice."

147

I looked back to the mirror again, fascinated. It wasn't exactly true that I was beautiful, although my eyes looked very bright, and my skin was nice, too, if anyone looked at me from a distance and couldn't see the freckles. How would it be having a baby? I wondered. How funny it would seem, being Leda Maude and having a romantic person like Alfred love her. Oh, love, love, beautiful, beautiful love!

"Peggy," I heard Mother call from downstairs. But she had not located me; no one had discovered what I had been doing. I slid guiltily from the room and ran into the bathroom, making a great deal of noise with the tap as though I were washing my hands, and then I went nonchalantly down the stairs, carrying Mrs. Mainwaring's glasses carefully in front of me.

Leda Maude had gone out in the yard, but when she saw a little band of women turning into the front yard she hurried indoors.

"Mother," she called hastily, "there's company coming. I'm going upstairs."

"You can't go upstairs, Leda Maude. It's you they're coming to see."

Mrs. Mainwaring looked very important and happy, like a huge deep-colored grape in her purple dotted swiss.

Although I had not been expressly invited to the shower, I took it for granted that I was to be a part of it. There were sixteen women, all friends of Leda

Maude's or her mother's. Some of the women had not seen Leda Maude's wedding ring yet, and she let them examine it carefully. It had two bands of diamonds across the front, set in yellow gold, instead of one band of diamonds or nothing but a narrow circlet of gold, like most of the women wore.

"We decided so suddenly to be married that we couldn't bother about an engagement ring, too," Leda Maude explained. "I thought I'd like this best anyway. It was Alfred's choice, too." And the diamonds flashed their hard little lights in the sun.

"Will Alfred be here soon, do you suppose?" The women settled themselves comfortably for talk on the sofa and worn overstuffed chairs and on the dining room chairs that Mother and Mrs. Mainwaring had brought in from the back of the house.

"Oh, yes." Leda Maude stared expectantly out of the window. "There's nothing would keep him away, in spite of his work, nothing at all."

As she spoke she looked out toward the lilac bush, whose lavender cones had burst into bloom, dozens of the tiny flowers opening to the sun. She gave a little gasp and her body seemed to turn and strain. Mrs. Mainwaring was beside her immediately, twisting the purple grape of herself out of shape as she bent over her anxiously.

"Are you all right, Leda Maude? Is anything the matter?"

"No, no really, Mother," and Leda Maude smiled wanly. "Everything's all right now."

Mother and Grandmother, who had been whispering together, went out of the room. Suddenly the ladies bent forward in their chairs and looked toward the door between the living room and dining room. Leda Maude turned, too. Mother and Grandmother were dragging a pink and white crepe paper covered bassinet, in which were piled gifts wrapped in tissue paper and tied with narrow pink baby ribbon, while the whole affair was presided over by a large cardboard stork carrying a tiny china doll. Everybody sat very still and self-conscious, waiting for Leda Maude to say something. Leda Maude only looked frightened.

"Don't be scared, child, they're for you." And her mother dragged the bassinet until it stood before Leda Maude.

"But I—I wasn't expecting—" Leda Maude's fingers trembled as she picked up a soft little package and untied the pink ribbon, which had been twisted into a fancy bow to look like a rose.

"Well, if you weren't expecting, Leda Maude," and her mother looked meaningfully at the little group, "these presents are going to be an awful mistake."

The whole group began to laugh merrily as Leda Maude held up a soft little flannel shirt so tiny that it looked like a doll's garment in her hands. There was a knitted cap and matching jacket of pale blue, with white ribbons run through the neck, a white sacque embroidered in pink and blue rosebuds, bootees, more little shirts, a downy blanket, a bright red cup with "Baby" lettered around the rim. At the bottom Leda Maude drew out a pale pink rattle, upon which was perched a lavender and blue stork with yellow eyes. Leda Maude stared at the rattle for a moment and then placed it on top of the pile of presents.

Mrs. Mainwaring let me pass around little slips of paper and pencils of all sizes. "It's for a game," she explained. "Everybody write a name, two names. One for a girl, one a boy's. Then we'll let Leda Maude choose."

The names were put in a box and shuffled around carefully. "I hope you draw the names I chose," Mrs. Mainwaring said gayly. "They'd be so fitting, one for grandpa Daniel Long Mainwaring, and—"

"Alfred, Jr., and Gwendolyn Mae," Leda Maude read softly from the two slips of paper that she drew from the box.

"Alfred will want it to be a boy, all right," Mother wagged her head wisely. "Men always do. And Junior will tickle him to death."

Gwendolyn Mae was the name I had written. I wanted to run up to Leda Maude and hug her and say, "Isn't it *fun*, oh, isn't it *wonderful* to be having a baby?" But suddenly I was too shy.

"If the baby looks like his father he'll grow up to be a movie star right enough," Leda Maude's Aunt Pearl giggled. "Is he really as handsome as his picture, Leda Maude?"

"I can't wait to see him in the flesh." Mrs. Mainwaring smiled at Leda Maude, as Mother and Aunt Pearl started toward the kitchen. "It was all such a surprise. Leda Maude didn't want to quit work or she would have told us sooner. I would have liked a big wedding myself."

The women drew into a little group about Leda Maude and began to ask her questions that I would have liked to hear, but Mother beckoned to me to come out in the kitchen to help her with refreshments. Mother was using her hand-painted plates. They were brought out only for company, and were filled now with strawberry shortcake and whipped cream.

Leda Maude looked tired. You could tell by the way her face was drawn, and every so often she would close her eyes as though to shut everyone out, although all around her the guests were taking second helpings and exclaiming about the gifts.

Finally, after everyone had gone, Leda Maude came slowly back into the living room from the porch, where she and her mother had said their final good-bys and thanks. The room was littered with tissue paper and ribbon and a few strawberry shortcake plates that had not been taken out. The little pile of presents was in the bassinet, and she picked them up carefully and turned toward the stairs. I started to pick up a piece of the pink and blue ribbon. I would ask Leda Maude if she wanted it, and if she didn't I would keep it. Mrs. Mainwaring came in from the hall smiling happily.

"My goodness, here's one of Leda Maude's presents on the floor," and she rescued a small flannel shirt that was tangled in a mass of tissue paper. "Mrs. Miller gave her that. She'd have a fit seeing it on the floor." She scooped up the tissue paper and some ribbon scraps and went upstairs, I following her with my bits of ribbon.

Leda Maude was down on her knees before the window in the bedroom.

"You dropped this when you picked up the presents," Mrs. Mainwaring said, placing the shirt with the pile that lay on Leda Maude's bed.

Leda Maude did not turn around. I stood in the doorway fingering my ribbon and wondering if I should ask Leda Maude now if she wanted the ribbon, or wait until Mrs. Mainwaring was not around. I looked at Leda Maude's dresser. It seemed somehow strange and bare. It was just the same and yet—

Mrs. Mainwaring must have noticed it, too.

"Why, Leda Maude, where's Alfred?" And she stared again at the dresser as though perhaps she might have overlooked the black and gold frame.

Leda Maude turned around slowly. She was holding the little pink rattle in her hand. She had not been crying, but there was something funny about her eyes. And now I could see Alfred in the gold and black frame lying beside her.

"He never was," she said slowly, wearily. "There never was an Alfred."

"Poor thing, light in her head, maybe it's almost her time," I heard Mrs. Mainwaring mutter, and she walked swiftly over to Leda Maude's side.

"Leda Maude, what's the matter? Get up from the floor and lie down on the bed. The afternoon's been too much for you."

I could tell she was frightened, and I began to be frightened, too. Leda Maude looked so strange and white, and her eyes stared far off into space, a distance into which I could not see. She did not move from the floor, only twirled the rattle about in her hand.

"I bought him from a photographer's store for a dollar, two dollars with the frame," Leda Maude breathed, and her voice was very even, very quiet. "The ring cost $200. All the savings I had. I wouldn't have asked Jim for a dime. Not after he married Donna. I wouldn't even tell him about the baby — but he knew."

"Leda Maude, have you gone mad?" There was panic in Mrs. Mainwaring's voice.

"Mad?" Leda Maude repeated vacantly.

Suddenly Mrs. Mainwaring began to cry. She knelt down beside Leda Maude, and laid her head on her shoulder, as if it were she, now, who were to be comforted, as if she were the daughter and Leda Maude her mother.

Leda Maude sat very still before the window, the rattle making a furious chopping noise in her hands, as though the lavender and blue stork with the yellow eyes would burst its sides with sound. Neither of them noticed me, and I stumbled from the doorway, the ribbon still crumpled in my hands. I went out in the yard by the lilac bush, and suddenly I, too, began to whimper, although I had no idea why. I held fiercely to a branch of the lilac, feeling the crush of blossoms under my hand. The pink and blue ribbon caught on the leaves and I left it hanging there when I went finally into the house.

"I wonder if Leda Maude will be coming down to the library tonight," I heard Mother asking Grandmother a little later. "All I want now is for that husband of hers to come get her and take her back to St. Louis before she has her baby right there in the *library*."

When I cried and cried for hours that night after I had gone to bed—was it because of Mrs. Mainwaring's tears, or my terror that Leda Maude would have her baby in the library, as Mother feared, or simply a nameless misery?—Mother said I must have eaten too many strawberries at the stork shower. So had Leda Maude or her mother, one or the other, Grandmother said wearily the next morning. "Somebody up there was crying all night long."

10

THE GYPSY BOY

Mr. Carnegie's Lib'ary was never the same to me after the gypsies came into it. It was as though the good, gray building had somehow been draped in tinsel and hung with Christmas tree ornaments, or something more strange and wonderful. I was only eleven or twelve during the gypsy episode and knew nothing of pagan myths and rituals, but even so I sensed that something much more ancient than Christmas had for a brief while collided with the library—only such a harsh term would seem to fit the appearance of these strangers from another world in the culture center of our small Midwestern town.

I would not be surprised if Mr. Carnegie glared disapprovingly at the gypsies from the respectability of his gilt frame the afternoon the brightly clad, rather dirty and noisy group of foreigners burst into his temple, jewelry clanking about the necks and at the ears of the women in a way that seemed somehow wicked. Everyone who saw the gypsies coming up the entrance steps stared, and one woman ran into the children's room to protect her child, who was innocently reading the Bobbsey Twins. It was well known that gypsies stole children. But Mother, the perfect hostess, although she must have been frightened to death, came out from behind the circulation desk and went to meet them, inquiring what they wanted. She knew it was not books.

They spoke in a language unknown to us all, with much waving of hands and darting of eyes about the building, but finally it became clear, from one of the men who spoke some English, that they had come to the wrong place—they were hunting the police station. One of the gypsy men had been arrested, which would certainly have been no surprise to any resident of Moberly, from what we knew of gypsies. His tribe had come to get him out; the library was a big important-looking building, perhaps the most impressive in town, thus the police —and the arrested gypsy—were probably in it.

After the gypsies had been directed to the police station—"They ought to have more sense than to go near that place, they'll *all* end up in jail"—there was much excitement and chattering from the patrons in the library. Everyone intended to go right home and lock his door, that was for sure. Mostly Moberly people did not lock doors, except for a few cautious ones like Mother. And even she, after carefully fastening the front door, hung the key neatly on a nail high up inside the screen, so that none of us coming home would ever be shut out. An extra key could even be found hanging from one of the flower boxes on the front porch, in case the one on the nail got lost. We all, nevertheless, felt well protected, guarded from all thieves, murderers, and kidnappers by the key.

As long as I could remember, I had heard of gypsies, but never before had I seen any so close. They came through town once or twice a year. We would hear a rumble of wagons going down Fourth Street, and looking out the back door we could see the brightly painted wooden gypsy wagons being drawn noisily out to their camp at the edge of town. They camped in the same field where carnivals were held, and circuses, so somehow they were always linked in my mind with these glittering, but not quite respectable, marvels. You would no more speak to a gypsy than to a carnival roustabout or circus worker. If you did, you were likely to be abducted and then you would spend the rest of your life in a gypsy caravan or a carnival show or under the Big Tent. All this was fine and exciting to talk about, and no one ever missed a circus or a carnival, but one would die rather than End Up That Way. It was somehow akin to Going To The Dogs, whatever *that* meant. The way gossips talked, plenty of people in town had Gone To The Dogs, even folks from good families who should know better.

At any rate, whenever the gypsy wagons rattled down Fourth Street, Eloise or Helen would cry out, "The gypsies, the gypsies!" and one of us would run to find Laddie and bring him in the house for safety — for of course gypsies also stole smart, valuable dogs.

Laddie had been named after President Harding's own dog, Laddie Boy, as well as Mr. Carnegie's favorite collie, so he was practically royal. The President's Laddie might have had his own valet and sat in on important Presidential meetings, and Mr. Carnegie's Laddie had lived in a Scottish castle, but our Laddie was just as pampered and adored. The White House Laddie once had a four-tiered cake of dog biscuits for his birthday party, and probably Mr. Carnegie's Laddie wore a gold and emerald collar, but our Laddie was given a platter of nut divinity on his birthday, and had pink ribbons tied about his paws and neck and tail to celebrate the occasion.

When the gypsies were in town we would lie in bed at night and frighten ourselves with tales of kidnapping, and Helen and Eloise, who were older and more knowledgeable, even hinted at worse. We would imagine the gypsies sitting around their campfires eating their strange, greasy food — this was Mother's contribution. To eat strange, greasy food was an abomination to her, and almost any meat was an abomination except a nice lean Swiss steak smothered in tomatoes and onions and potatoes, so you did not think of it as meat, or a delicate pink slice of baked ham, covered with pineapple and brown sugar — this we did not consider in the class with pork, which was not fit for a pig to eat — or a meat loaf, this, too, covered heavily with tomato sauce. Baked chicken was also acceptable when well surrounded by crisp dressing balls, home-pickled peaches, and parsley, so that we could not see its shape and remember its source.

No one in our family of women liked to think where meat came from. Somehow, if we ever considered the origin, it seemed almost as though we were eating Laddie, or old Fan, Mother's horse when she was a child, or Dickie Boy, *her* childhood dog. Mother was almost sorry she had not voted for Calvin Coolidge when she read he had made a pet of a raccoon that had been sent to him in the White House, instead of eating it for his Thanksgiving dinner, which was what the givers had intended. This showed he was particular about what he ate, just like we were.

Gypsies, for all we knew, ate their meat raw and might eat anything, even — and we would scream in horror — *Laddie*. Ah, how he was loved when the gypsies were in town; he was held in our arms, petted, given pieces of fudge and oatmeal cookies and even our own portions of Swiss steak or meat loaf. Just supposing the gypsies ever caught him!

Nothing was talked of at home the evening after

the gypsies came into the library but this amazing event. Mother had hastily gotten out all the clippings she had in the library collection about gypsy ways, and had put a picture of a gypsy cart, a gypsy dancer, and a gypsy camp on the display board. She had also found two or three books about gypsies that she arranged beneath it. She entitled the display "Children of Little Egypt," which she said was another name for them. She even planned to take down to the library her own water color of a gypsy girl that she had done when she was young. Her gypsy girl did not look at all like the women who came into the library; she looked, as a matter of fact, something like Mother herself, Anglo-Saxon, clean, completely bowdlerized. Nevertheless she was wearing gold hoop earrings and carrying a tambourine, and she would most assuredly fit into the display.

The news of the gypsies in the library was all over town before Mother had left for the evening, and one or two of the women's clubs were already planning to have gypsy programs, with somebody singing "Tell Me, Little Gypsy" and "Gypsy Love Song." Mother decided to ask Miss Everhart, my elocution teacher, to try to find a reading about gypsies for me to learn, so I could dress up in my Halloween costume—it was a sort of gypsy dress, as Mother and I envisaged gypsies—and give a recitation at her Thursday Club. With my costume I always wore brass curtain rings which were attached to rubber bands curled around my ears, and I carried a tambourine hung with bright ribbons, like the lady in Mother's painting.

The information about gypsies that Mother had dug out of her clipping collection was fascinating. In Spain gypsies lived in caves, from singles to twenty-room affairs, and they even had their stores, schools, and churches in the caves. This made them, in my mind, somehow akin to the prehistoric cave men who wore bear and leopard skins, and thus all the more exciting and fearful. In Central Europe many gypsies played a musical instrument called a dulcimer, which had been invented in Persia or Arabia. Our own piano was descended from it.

Usually gypsies came and went so quickly that no one knew when they had left. For a day or two a gypsy lady might come to a house and ask to read fortunes, but usually their stay in one place was a brief one. On this visit they lingered. It was probably, Mother said, because of the gypsy in jail. Anyway, one saw little groups of them walking about the streets, and the townsfolk glowered and said to each other it was time for these foreigners to be moving on. Other men worked for a living.

Nevertheless, although no one liked gypsies in the flesh, everyone seemed to love them in the library display and as objects of school and club programs. Mother had been complimented frequently on her gypsy display, and said this proved one should save everything about *everything*, just as she had always maintained. Certainly no one would ever have dreamed gypsies would suddenly be so popular—on paper, that is. They were much more romantic when one read about them than when one actually met them, or *smelled* them!

I was alone in the periodical room the evening the Gypsy Boy came into it. For a moment I was frightened and wondered if I should call out "Help, gypsies!" but then I saw that *he* was frightened. He gazed around him in bewilderment, as though at any moment he would dart out of the room. I had never seen a gypsy alone before. I was not my mother's daughter for nothing, however; I, too, knew the amenities of a junior hostess in the library. As I walked over to the boy, I thought at first that he was going to run away from me, but after shifting from one foot to another he stood his ground and stared at me.

"Can I help you find something?" I asked him, hoping Mother would not see him and come in to share my glory of a tête-à-tête with a real, live gypsy. It was possible, of course, that he spoke only gypsy language, and that, I knew from the library display, was ancient Sanskrit or Prakrit.

The boy, who must have been about fourteen years of age, only muttered, so I could not tell whether he was thinking in English or Sanskrit, but he looked curiously at the magazines spread out on the long tables. I suddenly noticed that he was very handsome, and now it was I who became shy.

Sensing this, he grew bolder, more assured, and picked up a magazine that had a picture of a horse on the cover.

"I've a better horse than this," he said scornfully. He spoke roughly, but I could understand him well. His English was not at all like the broken English used by the man who had spoken to Mother the day the gypsy group came into the library. I remembered now that this boy had been with the group, standing in the back.

"Where are you from?" I asked, which was the standard question employed by any Moberly person wishing to establish contact with an outsider. If he said St. Louis, I could say "I have an aunt there," and thus a bond would be formed. Or if he said Kansas City, I could say "I've been there." Without such a mutual bond, conversation was usually impossible. There was nothing else to tie two people together, as far as I knew, because I certainly could not ask "What school do you go to?" which was another good bond-welder. Gypsies did not go to school.

"Everywhere," the boy answered me shortly.

This was a strange and frightening and yet wonderful answer. I saw him wandering through Rumania, Russia, and Hungary. Possibly he had even lived in the caves of Spain.

"What would you like to read?" I inquired politely. We did not have newspapers from Everywhere in the library, but we did have *The New York*

Times, of course, as well as the *Chicago Tribune*, the *Kansas City Star*, and the *Christian Science Monitor*. Or maybe he even wanted to see if the arrest of the gypsy was in the *Moberly Monitor-Index*.

"I can't read," he said savagely. I looked at him in surprise. Why was he in the library then? He picked up the magazine with the horse's picture on it again, and thumbed through the pages, still muttering, "I can't read."

He finally threw the magazine down on the table in disgust, saying, "Oh, it's all just words," and without even saying good-by to me stalked out of the room and out of the library.

Mother saw him as he went down the entrance stairs and she came running into the periodical room.

"That was one of the *gypsies*," she said excitedly. "And you were in here all alone!"

"He speaks English just like everybody else," I said, somehow feeling superior even to my own mother. "And he's been Everywhere."

"You know you don't talk to strangers," Mother reminded me severely, and I could see she was frightened.

"When they're in the library they're not strangers," I responded, parroting words she had always used before. "They're library patrons."

"Oh," Mother cried out in exasperation, "gather up the magazines. It's almost time to close up. And high time, too," she concluded, stalking out of the periodical room. Gypsies safely on the display board, and gypsies talking to her own child, were two different things, as even a foolish daughter ought to know.

Nothing could have kept me away from the library the next night. I went directly to the periodical room, taking my schoolwork with me, but I kept watching for the Gypsy Boy. This time he did not seem frightened as he entered the room, and again I was lucky. Mother, who had been watching for him just as I had, had received a phone call in the office and did not see him enter.

"What's all those men in a boat out there?" he asked curiously, motioning toward the entry room.

"Men in a boat?" I repeated stupidly.

"Out there in the hall, up on the wall, a man's standing up in a boat, like he's going to jump out or something."

"Oh," I said, relieved, "that's George Washington."

I thought everybody knew what George Washington looked like, even gypsies. The Gypsy Boy honestly must be pretty dumb.

"Well, what's he standing up in a boat for like that?"

You would think, the way he talked, that it was George Washington who was dumb.

"Why, he's crossing the Delaware, of course. He and his soldiers."

Then I remembered that the Gypsy Boy had never

been to school. He might not even know who George Washington was if he came from Spain or India. But he had lost interest in George Washington now. It was obvious he had never heard of him before.

I had gathered a pile of magazines that I thought the Gypsy Boy might want to look at. One was an issue of *Theatre Arts* in which I had found a photograph of gypsy dancers. Another was a journal filled with horses and other livestock. And another had photographs of castles. If the Gypsy Boy had been Everywhere, he had probably seen castles.

"I thought you'd like to see some pictures," I told him shyly.

This time he sat down at the table beside me, like any other library patron, and began to thumb through the magazines. The gypsies in *Theatre Arts* made him laugh. His brown eyes twinkled and he turned to me and said cheerfully, "They're not gypsies."

"It says they are," I argued defensively.

"I know gypsies," he answered me, still good-humoredly, and he became absorbed in the magazine with the castles. He said nothing about these pictures, but looked at them for a long while. They seemed to interest him as much as the horses.

"Don't you want to read?" I asked him, finally. "Can't you ever stay anyplace long enough to learn to read?"

"What would I do with reading?" he said.

"But the way you talk," I answered, "it's different from the others. You talk like—well, like people talk who read a lot. And you're in a library, that means you want to read."

He got up quickly from the table and was suddenly angry. "I don't want to read. Gypsies don't have time to read."

He and Mother passed each other in the doorway of the periodical room.

"When will those no-account gypsies ever leave town?" she said angrily. "I never knew gypsies to hang around a place so long."

She took her painting of the gypsy girl home that night from the library, but she did not hang it up again over the buffet. Instead she announced she was tired of looking at it, and that she never had thought it was much good, anyway.

The boy did not come into the library the next night, and Mother said he was probably in jail, just like the other gypsy. Or maybe the gypsies had left town finally. She dismantled the gypsy display and put up one about Beautiful Switzerland.

I supposed the boy had left town, too, but I knew he was not in jail. And in case he was still about, I continued to come on down to the library at night, telling Mother I had to get material for a theme. I looked carefully through the magazine about castles that he had liked. We had a bond now, we could always talk about castles, even if I didn't know much about Everywhere and he didn't know who

George Washington was.

Finally, one night when I looked up from my book, the Gypsy Boy was standing beside me.

"We're leaving tomorrow," he said. "I've come to look at the pictures again."

I deluged him with magazines, the new *National Geographic*, anything with pictures, and he kept muttering with pleasure as I brought them to him. Suddenly I knew Mother was standing at the table watching him. I stared at her, fearful that she would snatch the magazines from his hands, which, it was true, were dirty. And it was just as true that he smelled of horses, and grease, and strangeness. We were both very quiet as we stared at each other, I in fear, and Mother—I don't know what Mother was thinking. But all at once I knew we were sharing a bond, Mother and I, over the Gypsy Boy. Mother even smiled at him, and said she hoped he was enjoying the magazines. This startled him, and he got up quickly from his chair and pushed the magazines away from him, staring at Mother with hostility. She was Enemy, she was a grown-up Outsider. I was too young to matter, but Mother belonged to the people who put gypsies in jail.

As he started to leave the room Mother picked up an armful of the magazines. "Take them with you," she said. "Take them and keep them."

She was breaking a rule and she knew it. Those magazines belonged to the library, and she herself would have to buy new ones to replace them.

They were new magazines and no one could even check them out until the next ones came, and here she was *giving* them away to a gypsy boy who could not read. He did not bother to thank her, only grabbed them as though he was afraid she would snatch them away from him, and he ran out the door.

"Just let anyone say anything to me about this and he'll wish he hadn't," Mother said furiously, staring after the Gypsy Boy. "Here's a room full of magazines you can't get folks to read, but sure as you know, someone will be asking tomorrow for just the ones that boy has under his arm."

Neither of us talked about the Gypsy Boy as we walked home that night. I kept wondering what the other gypsies would think when he came back to the camp with magazines, and I wished he knew that people should always wash their hands before they touched books and magazines.

The gypsies left town the next day. Usually they sped away at dawn, but this time it was late afternoon and I was just coming home from school. As the wagons rumbled up Fourth Street, several other children coming home from school called out "The gypsies!" and started running to their homes.

I stood very still on the corner so that I could see every wagon. The Gypsy Boy was driving the last one in the caravan, an older gypsy man sitting beside him. I know he saw me because he looked directly at me, but he did not show any recognition at all. I suddenly realized I did not even know his name; I could not tell him good-by. I ran along beside the wagon, calling out to him, "My name is Peggy, what's yours? We never told our names!" But the Gypsy Boy would not look at me. He kept his eyes straight ahead, and the caravan went so swiftly that soon all of the wagons were out of sight.

That evening at home nothing could please me. I complained that the supper was awful; I hated my new coat; my teacher, whom I had always before loved, was mean to me; and my throat was sore. Finally I cried. I heard Mother telling Grandmother she did not know what would become of me, the way I carried on about everything. Grandmother, who was very wise, said to remember that I was starting to grow up, and probably there was a boy around somewhere who was causing me to act this way.

In all of my life I have had three marvelous rides. None of them have been in automobiles, although I have ridden in fancy Buicks, and even an old Model T Ford, and in the rumble seat of a roadster when I was in college. I drive a neat blue Chevrolet now, but I am careless about keeping the chrome trim gleaming, and a dent or two and chipped paint do not trouble me. This simply does not matter. All I ever really care about are the three rides that have been important to me.

One was the ride I had in the Dethier girls' buggy when I was very young. The Dethier girls had the last buggy in town, and since they lived on the edge of town — actually not too far from the field where the gypsies camped — they had a barn and a meadow for their beautiful brown horse. The fact that the world had entered the automobile age did not seem to bother them at all. When they came to town to shop they hitched their horse to the buggy and rode in proudly. The automobile age did not bother their horse, either. While the girls shopped, he stood calmly among the Fords and fancier cars, switching his feathery tail back and forth to keep the flies off of his glossy brown hide. Summer and winter he wore a straw hat trimmed with daisies so the sun or the cold would not beat down upon his head. There were little holes in it for his ears to poke through. His hat was decorated with flags on the Fourth of July and with holly or tinsel around Christmas time.

One day when the Dethier girls had been in the library and had checked out an armful of books, I helped them carry the books out to their buggy.

"Get in for a ride," said the wonderful Dethier girls, who were probably well in their seventies at this time.

I climbed up on the slick, shiny, black seat in front beside Miss Martha, and embarked on the first marvelous ride of my life. I can remember to this day the black fringe swinging gently back and forth from the top of the buggy as we rode down the street, and the careful clop, clopping of the horse — no one had to tell *him* where to go. He had an established, well-regulated world extending from one end of Fourth Street, where he lived, to the other end, where the stores and library and church were located and where he trotted once or twice a week.

For the first time in my life I had truly entered another age, another world; I was seeing Moberly through eyes that were not my own as we rode slowly down the street. This was how my grandmother had ridden about Moberly long before I was born, and how my mother had sat behind old Fan when she was a girl. I slid back and forth on the shiny seat, bumping up and down in rhythm with the buggy's motion, and admired the way the horse's tail swung back and forth, just as rhythmically, as he hurried homeward. When we arrived at the Dethier girls' home they allowed me to help them unhitch their horse, take off his straw hat, and give him a lump of sugar, which was his usual treat following an afternoon's outing.

The second marvelous ride was in Mr. Hank Berry's cart. Mr. Berry, like the Dethier girls, did not allow the age of the automobile to trouble him. He had a little brown and white pony and a cart, and since he owned land near our house and frequently went there to do some work on it, I was well acquainted with the little pony named Toby, whom I had often patted lovingly. On one unforgettable day Mr. Berry invited me for a ride. This was nothing at all like the Dethier girls' buggy. The little cart was used for hauling things — it was a rough farm wagon — but Mr. Berry actually allowed me to sit in the driver's seat and hold the reins of the pony as we traveled through town.

Just as Mr. Berry was not the aristocrat that the Dethier girls were, so his pony did not have the excellent manners of the Dethier girls' horse. He smelled slightly of manure, his coat was rough, and there were tangles in his mane. But like the Dethier girls' horse, the little pony knew exactly where he was going; no one had to say *giddap* or *whoa*, and certainly never had to use the whip. Surely no one would *ever* use a whip on a dear little pony. I saw five of my friends, including Jack Nevins, as I rode about town, and they saw me. Jack yelled in admiration for all the world to hear, "Hey, look at *that*, would you? Look who's getting to drive!" When we returned home Mr. Berry said I had handled the pony like a real horse trainer, and the pony himself bared his teeth in a sort of smile, and whinnied as though he loved me.

The third marvelous ride has taken place only in my mind, but nevertheless it is just as real as the other two, and as unforgettable. It is a ride in a gypsy wagon.

I am standing on Fourth Street when the gypsies come through town. First there is a rumbling sound, like faraway, menacing thunder, followed by shrill, frightened cries of "Gypsies, gypsies, run!" and the frantic barking of a little dog who leaps against me, warning me to flee from danger. And then I see the caravan rolling toward me, terrifying and yet irresistible, the strangeness of another world threatening all that I have known and valued, and yet offering some marvelous enticement. The Gypsy Boy is riding in the first wagon, a green one, painted with all colors. He sees me standing by the curb and calls his horse to a stop and invites me to jump in. I climb up on the hard wooden seat beside him, neither of us speaking, and we ride swiftly down the street, out to the gypsy camp. His eyes, which stare at me curiously from time to time, are dark and foreign, and they have looked upon remote and wondrous countries that I have never seen, only dreamed of, or imagined. His hands holding the reins are brown and hard, and when one of them closes over mine briefly I know that we are sharing a bond pledged long ago, in remembrance of enchanted castles, and a pile of old, dog-eared magazines, greasy and torn from much handling, still bearing the faded stamp of Mr. Carnegie's Lib'ary.

I look back into the dark and mysterious interior of the wagon and see that it is full of all kinds of things: sacks, a mattress, an iron pot, a tambourine, gaudy jewelry, even an evil-looking old woman fingering a pack of dirty cards. As we drive beyond the town and into the camp I see a great fire blazing and a group of gaily dressed gypsies singing and dancing, and little children romping about. Someone is playing a dulcimer. I have left Moberly now forever and am no longer Peggy Elsea, the librarian's daughter. Not even Mr. Carnegie himself could bring me back. I am a gypsy.

11

THE SHOWCASE

With luck, Mother often told Grandmother, the Misses Bynner would leave their Showcase to the library when they died. That was where it belonged, where everybody could see it, not hidden away for two elderly spinsters to spend all their time moping over it.

"I've seen Miss Letty work a whole morning just rearranging the letters in it and polishing the glass doors. I wouldn't even be surprised," she added irreverently, "if they said their prayers in front of it."

The fact that Mother thought the Showcase should be in the library showed how public-spirited and unselfish she was, because the truth is, she was proud that the case reposed in her own house — in our apartment rented by Miss Letty and Miss Emily Bynner.

The Misses Bynner had known a Famous Artist.

Everyone in town was aware of that. Mother, of course, knew all about him. She had books about his paintings at the library, and considered him special not just because the art critics said so, but because he had been a friend of the Misses Bynner. The Famous Artist was dead now, had been, in fact, for forty years, and the Misses Bynner were old and lean and always looked to me as though they were hungry, but they still had crowded into their parlor a big boxy glass showcase filled with letters and postcards and a few sketches signed by the Artist they had known when they were young and he was still a nobody.

Before the Misses Bynner moved into our apartment they had lived for years in a shapeless brown wooden house that looked like a huge chocolate that had been stepped on and mangled out of shape; it rambled over a big yard clotted with scraggly bushes and sick-looking trees. Shingles were forever dangling from the roof, and the Bynner girls' very ancient papa was always sitting on the shabby front porch wrapped up in a plaid wool shawl, even when it was summer. You could hear his hack hack of a cough all the way down the block. Once when I had gone past the Bynner house with Jack Nevins, Jack had yelled, "Take off your long underwear, mister, it's summertime." Then he had become frightened and had run down the street, and I became frightened, too, for some reason, although Papa did not seem to have heard, and I ran down the street after him, leaving behind us Papa's hack hack.

Then Papa died, and the Misses Bynner sold their squashed chocolate and came to live upstairs, glass showcase and all. Although our apartment was furnished, they brought some of their own furniture along, too: stiff black horsehair chairs, a rosewood table, and a great mahogany desk. These things crowded the little apartment, but they seemed to provide the proper background for the Showcase.

Mother helped them arrange the Showcase and often brought them home copies of stories she saw in the city papers and in magazines about the Artist. She always spoke of them as the Misses Bynner, never Miss Emily and Miss Letty, but as though they were a joint person, and she was extremely proud of their cultural, although now long terminated, association with a famous personage.

It was really Miss Letty who had been the Artist's friend. Miss Emily had known him, too, Mother said, but it was Miss Letty with whom the Artist had been — well, Miss Letty had never actually said so, but you could tell from the way she talked, and the things she held back when she spoke about him, that the Artist had been in love with her.

"If he loved her, why didn't he marry her?" I was very curious. I could not imagine Miss Letty Bynner being loved by anyone. I still remembered a time one spring when I had picked a snowball flower from her bush for a May basket, and she had leaned out of the window, calling sharply, "Drop those flowers this instant, little girl, and don't let me see you taking our flowers again."

"Probably because of old Mr. Bynner's getting sick. She used to study music, she and Miss Emily both, in St. Louis, and that's where they met him. Then old Mr. Bynner lost most of his money and got sick, and they had to come home. And right after that the Artist died. The Misses Bynner never would play the piano for anyone after they came back. All that time in St. Louis studying music, and you'd never know they knew one note from another to look at them. Just frittered their lives away after that, making such a big thing of that Showcase."

Miss Letty and Miss Emily did not like each other. No one had told me this, and when I said so to Mother one day she told me indignantly that I was dreaming. But I knew—I knew because of the way Miss Emily muttered when Miss Letty was taking a bath: "She's *still* in the tub, just lying there soaking, when there's six others in this house might want to come in." She would finger her bar of white soap and her washcloth made from parts of one of her papa's old undershirts, and walk out into the hall every so often to see if Miss Letty had opened the bathroom door yet, although of course she knew she hadn't. And I knew because of the way Miss Letty said angrily, although not too loudly, when it was Miss Emily's turn to cook their supper: "Cooking in butter again, all that butter gone to waste, when lard would do. Her and her appetite."

She was always talking about Miss Emily's appetite, the fancy things Miss Emily liked, and she grew particularly incensed over Miss Emily's love of maraschino cherries. Maraschino cherries were delicacies that should have been definitely in the luxury class, something to be used sparingly at holiday time or for company, their round redness cut up into infinitesimal bits for garnish, so that the bottle would last a long while. But Miss Emily liked to eat them as casually as though they were fruit balls from the dime store, although she must have eaten them so hastily when she had them — fearing the scorn of Miss Letty's eyes and tongue — that they afforded her little pleasure.

I was fascinated by their wonderful Showcase with its letters and postcards and sketches, laid out on a dark red velvet background, with a picture of the Artist in the middle of it all. Neither of them seemed to mind my looking at it. The only thing Miss Letty resented was when Miss Emily would tell me about a particular letter or card in the case, and then Miss Letty would say stiffly, "The real story of that letter is a little different, Peggy, Emily isn't acquainted with the truth of it. What really happened was this."

And she would tell me another story of the letter's history, although Miss Emily said nothing, only growing very red and biting her nails all the while Miss Letty talked. But afterward Miss Emily would draw me aside when Miss Letty was not around and whisper hurriedly, "It *is* true what I told you; I know as well as she does." She would look as though she were going to cry, and somehow I always believed her; I guess because I liked her much better than Miss Letty.

Mother's Thursday Club program was solved immediately when the Misses Bynner moved upstairs. She would present a program on modern art, and have the Misses Bynner as guest speakers on the Artist, illustrating their talks with firsthand glimpses at the trophies in their Showcase. Not that such programs had not been given many times in the past by various groups, but the Misses Bynner had gotten a little cranky about their Showcase in the last few years and did not give a program for just anybody anymore. Miss Letty was said to have remarked from time to time that she might write a book about the Artist herself, and not give away all she knew for free. She often came down to the library and looked through the material about him that Mother had accumulated in the clipping file. Mother worried that Miss Letty even "borrowed" some of the clippings when no one was looking, but of course she did not want to be so rude as to come right out and say so. Miss Letty was an important person because of her association with the Artist, and besides she had a caustic tongue. Mother comforted herself with the thought that anyway the material would ultimately all come back to the library, along with the Showcase, when the Misses Bynner died.

"I've asked both of them to make talks," Mother confided to the Thursday Club program chairman, "because I wouldn't want to hurt Miss Emily's feelings. But I'm sure it's really Miss Letty who has all the information, and of course she was the Artist's — friend," she finished delicately. And then, knowingly, "Just imagine the things she could tell us about him if she really wanted to, little inside things none of the world knows or maybe even guesses at." Mother sighed. "But I guess that's too much to hope for. I'm sure I've wanted to keep some secrets about Luther, and I know you don't want to tell everything you know about your husband." Not, of course, that the Artist had been Miss Letty's husband, but for all anyone knew, although it was wicked even to think it, he might have been her *lover*.

I was as proud of the Showcase as Mother was, and, with such glory this close to me, I planned to write a theme about the Artist for my English class. With none of my mother's delicacy, I asked Miss Emily what he truly had looked like.

"Like a poet, a dreamer," she said reflectively, "a sensitive soul wounded by life's harshness."

"Nonsense," said Miss Letty quickly. "He was like a Greek soldier. Put a helmet on him and he'd have looked as though he were leading an army to victory."

They glared at each other, and I stared at the picture in the middle of the Showcase. I could not see that he was like a soldier *or* a poet. He had a droopy mustache and long sideburns and a little beard, and it was not easy to see, with all that hair, what he had looked like.

Soon there was much bustling and cleaning going on all over the house in readiness for the Thursday Club meeting. The business session was to be held downstairs in our living room, where the refreshments were later to be served, and Mother's introduction to the program would be given there, too, but at some point the ladies would all troop up to the Misses Bynner's parlor to gaze at the Showcase and have the Misses Bynner point out special letters and sketches to them. Both Mother and the Misses Bynner cleaned and polished every surface that was polishable. Mother made dozens of little ribbon sandwiches and angel food cake and peach ice cream. She got out her best embroidered linen napkins and had me polish the silver and pick mint for the lemonade. The Misses Bynner went over every inch of their Showcase, although since they performed this rite almost daily, it was unlikely that there was any dirt on the glass doors and the mahogany legs and frame. Miss Letty fussed about with the red velvet, and Miss Emily said they ought to put a new lining inside and make it blue for a change, but Miss Letty said, outraged, that the lining had always been red and this was the color the Artist liked best, anyway.

"Blue," said Miss Emily stubbornly. "His eyes were blue, and he always wore blue ties. And there were all those blues he used in his paintings."

Miss Letty always won the arguments, though. And the Showcase would have looked funny if they'd changed the velvet, since the letters had lain on that red since the day the Misses Bynner fixed it up.

The letters were mostly to Miss Letty, and although none of them, as far as anyone knew, were true, downright love letters, they showed he thought a great deal of her and valued her judgment of his work. There were a few postcards to Miss Emily stuck in the Showcase, as an afterthought, it seemed, and no one but Miss Emily herself usually paid much attention to them.

"No one knew or cared anything about him when he wrote those letters and made those sketches," Mother said. "It was ten years after he died before people began making a fuss over his work and saying he was great. And I still don't think Miss Letty knows much about painting, for all he gave those sketches to her."

Mother, of course, did. She might not be in a class with the Artist, but her hand-painted china and water colors were a credit to anybody.

The program would not be any novelty to me, since I had heard so much about the history of each of the items in the Showcase, but Mother said I should come: I might get some new ideas for my

English theme. Miss Letty just might say something new, even if she made it up.

"That's not very kind," Grandmother admonished her, but her eyes were twinkling. We all knew Miss Letty was histrionic and liked to embroider her stories.

Miss Letty opened the program with the part about the Artist looking like the Greek soldier—I could see that picture appealed to her very much, and as she talked Miss Emily looked down at the floor, and kept tapping her foot nervously. Miss Letty fluttered the letters, handling them as though they were butterflies' wings. One or two she let the ladies touch, but the rest she kept firmly in her own hand, reading the messages clearly and proudly.

"This," she said finally, "was the last letter I had from him. Emily and I had come back home, you know, to look after Papa. I never dreamed, of course, when I left St. Louis that day, that I should never see him again, that in two months he would be—" she paused dramatically—"dead."

"It's been forty years or more since he died," Mother had said to Grandmother earlier in the day, "and I sometimes think they believe it happened yesterday. Luther's been gone only six years. Do you think it will be like this for me thirty-four years from now?" She was momentarily a mother I did not know at all, anguish changing her from mother into woman, a transformation difficult for a child to comprehend. As Miss Letty spoke the word "dead," she, too, seemed to undergo this same terrible transformation, not old, cross Miss Letty, but anguished woman.

Miss Emily, rather rudely, had slipped out of the room as Miss Letty was talking. After Miss Letty had finished, and was standing regally and silently before the Showcase, Miss Emily returned, holding a little silken packet in her hand, pressed to her chest.

"Miss Emily will talk to us now," the Thursday Club president said, smiling, and rapping gently with a tiny gavel. "Miss Emily . . . ."

"Here," Emily gasped, thrusting the little silken packet into the surprised hands of the president. Suddenly she was sniffling, and Letty was hissing "Emily," and twenty pairs of eyes were staring, fascinated.

Mrs. Harwick, the president, did not quite know what to do with the little packet, and she held it uneasily, smiling a little uncertainly at Miss Emily.

"There's a letter to me inside of it," Miss Emily said finally, and she looked almost as though she wished she had it back, but by this time Mrs. Harwick had opened it up.

"Why—it's from *him*," she said, puzzled, "but it says, it says—" She stumbled over her words and looked up at Emily, surprised. "It's signed by the Artist," she floundered.

"Give it back," Emily whispered suddenly, looking as though she wanted to run away.

"Give it *here*," said Miss Letty, grabbing the letter out of Mrs. Harwick's hands.

Then, to the horror and delight of the Thursday Club, Miss Letty and Miss Emily fought. Miss Emily tried to snatch the bit of paper out of Miss Letty's hands. Miss Letty cried out, "Emily, you fool!" and Miss Emily screamed angrily, "It's mine, it's mine, it's always been mine. Richard wrote it to *me*!"

It certainly had never been in the Showcase, the Thursday Club members all agreed afterward over their ribbon sandwiches and angel food cake and ice cream. Naturally the Misses Bynner had not come downstairs, although Mother had hastily announced, in the midst of the fighting, that refreshments were ready to be served there. Mrs. Harwick, the only one who had seen Miss Emily's letter, kept repeating what she had read in it that instant before Miss Letty had grabbed it away from her.

"Why, there's nothing in the Showcase like *that*. It must have been Miss Emily he was in love with. That's what he said, right there in black and white. He said Letty or no Letty, he was mad about *her*, Emily, and they'd work it out some way. Just give him time."

"That's what he didn't have," Mother said solemnly. "What do you suppose would have happened if he hadn't died right after that?" But no one, of course, had the answer to that.

"I don't quite know what to say to either of them when I see them after all this," Mother said finally, a little uneasily. "Do you suppose that letter will go in the Showcase, too?"

The Showcase was smashed sometime in the middle of the night. It was a terrible sound coming out of the dark, and for a few minutes Mother and Helen and Eloise and I just lay in our beds, afraid to speak or to move. Laddie was carrying on like a mad dog. Then Mother, who was always brave in emergencies, got up and turned on all the lights. She made us get dressed, and would have sent one of us over to the Nevinses' to get help if it were not such an ungodly hour. Since the phone was opposite the upstairs apartment, that was no help.

At last we all marched up the stairs, Mother and Laddie leading the way, my sisters and I creeping in terror behind her. When Mother knocked on the Misses Bynner's door, no one answered her, and she opened it herself. Both Miss Emily and Miss Letty were standing beside the Showcase. There was glass all over the parlor floor. Miss Letty had a long gash on her right arm from the shattered glass, and she kept sticking her hands into that mess of glass and velvet, poking around the letters. Emily was moaning and crying, and holding a piece of red velvet against her as though it contained her heart. She had blood on her face.

Mother did not quite know what to do, besides sending Helen downstairs for alcohol and gauze and tape to fix Miss Letty's arm and Miss Emily's face, and telling Eloise to bring up some tea or lemonade or milk or *something* – although why she thought anyone would want to eat or drink at a time like this, she admitted afterward, she had no idea. Strangely enough, so strong is social custom when one is presented with food, Miss Emily and Miss Letty sat down quietly in the midst of all the wreckage, and Mother served them some of the ribbon sandwiches and cake and ice cream that were left from the club refreshments, and that Eloise thought would restore law and order to the Misses Bynner's life. They ate as though they were little toy dolls wound up and supposed to take first the sandwich, then the cake, then the lemonade, until their mechanism had run down. Mother got the broom and dustpan and a big wastebasket and began to sweep the glass into a huge pile, while the Misses Bynner sat there watching her, nobody saying a word. Finally, when Mother said, "You'd both better go to bed now and get a good night's sleep," not realizing how ridiculous this sounded, they went meekly into their bedroom without a backward glance at the Showcase.

"No point in spreading tales around about all this," Mother cautioned us severely, when we had gone back downstairs. "Somebody knocked against that case in the dark, that's how it happened."

Of course she knew we knew better. There was a hammer on the floor, and there were even hammer marks on the beautifully waxed mahogany legs of the Showcase. The whole thing had been battered by someone so that nothing would be left of it. The Artist's picture was nowhere to be seen, but the letters were strewn all over the floor, torn into tiny pieces. None of us could tell if Miss Emily's letter was there, too, but on the floor there were bits of a silken packet, like the one in which she had hidden her letter all those years.

"There's your proof," Mother said grimly several days later, "that the Showcase should have been safely down in the library, just as I said it should. You can't depend on people to guard their treasures."

She sighed heavily and looked around at her own precious antique blue and milk glass, and her hand-painted china, probably seeing her daughters, or their daughters, at some future, terrible time, smashing it angrily to the floor for one reason or another, or possibly for no reason at all.

"The funny thing is," I heard her telling Mrs. Nevins, "the Misses Bynner somehow seem happier now that the Showcase is gone. I even heard Miss Letty say she might play the organ for the Baptist Church choir—after all these years when she wouldn't go near a piano. I suppose they'll be wanting to drag a piano up there now to take the place of the Showcase. And Miss Emily's got herself some paints and asked if she could copy some of my water colors. You'd think, wouldn't you, if she copied anybody's work it would be *his*."

12

A VERY CULTURED FAMILY

Mother thought very highly of Mrs. Reginald Garson because she read the best books in the library, none of the light popular fiction, or mysteries, or Westerns, but the good important works, biography and history and a smattering of poetry.

Mother tried to remember that Mr. Carnegie had not scorned popular fiction for the library shelves. He had even remarked concerning the inclusion of such books in libraries that it was no use to provide a ladder with the first rung so high that the weak could not use it. The first step, he warned, should be near to the ground and very easy. Mother obediently followed Mr. Carnegie's advice and patiently aided her library readers to make their first tottering steps with such treats as Edgar Rice Burroughs and Zane Grey. She could not help admiring, however, patrons like Mrs. Garson who had long ago leaped to the top rung in her literary wanderings.

"She has a fine mind," Mother told people proudly when the Garsons decided to rent our apartment. Although it was of no consequence to our neighbors that Mother catered to tenants with minds, it mattered to Mother herself to know that she did not want just anybody with rent money — even if, unfortunately, beggars and landladies could not always be choosers.

"They're a very cultured family," Mother warned us before the Garsons arrived, "so watch your manners. I went to school with some of the Garsons, and the whole family is cultured and refined."

The Garsons sounded dreadful. Who wanted anyone upstairs who was *that* refined? Eloise and I regarded it as a catastrophe — we had adored Myrtle Shanks — and even Helen waited apprehensively for the Garsons to move in, although she said haughtily that she would be glad to have cultured people, too.

"Are there any children?" I asked, remembering unpleasantly how Herb and Benny Friedhoff had invaded my bush cave and broken my clover houses.

"A little boy, a nice, quiet little boy," Mother said. "He's their grandson. His mother is a college graduate and is teaching in Chicago, but Billy lives with his grandparents." Nobody seemed to know exactly where Sam Hopper, Billy's father, was living, excepting that it was not Chicago.

The Garsons looked terribly cultured the day they moved upstairs. Mrs. Reginald Garson — somehow one would never think of referring to her as just Mrs. Garson, without that Reginald tacked on to it — was rather dowdy in appearance, but she carried herself majestically and wore imposing, cultured-looking hats. Mr. Garson — he did not seem to need the Reginald — was several inches shorter than his wife and he looked very fierce. The little grandson was five years old and had curly red hair. He seemed shy when his grandparents introduced him and would not say a word; he just grinned and grinned.

They were quiet enough, quieter, I guess, than anyone we had ever had before, and Mother thought that at last she had gotten the perfect family, the one that all landladies dream of. Mother confessed to a secret shame for Mrs. Reginald Garson, however. In spite of her fine mind and her preference for good literature, she adored the game of bridge. She played it frequently and well, her excellent mind relaxed for the moment in the biography of the king, the deuce, and the ace — the beginning of disintegration, not of morals, as the Methodist Church had believed when Mother was young, but of culture and the brain.

In her abhorrence of cultural time-wasting, Mother was akin, although she did not know it, to the nineteenth-century English bibliomaniac Sir Thomas Phillipps, who could not bear that anyone should give to gameplaying or any such idle pursuit a moment that could better be devoted to books.

Our house, too, had a resemblance to that of the eccentric Sir Thomas, not in its magnificence but in its frightening accumulation of cultural treasures to be preserved for posterity, even if the occupants were pushed aside. In Mother's case, the treasures were not only books but antique glassware, none of it spread daintily about to hold candy or just to look pretty, as in most correct households I visited, but dishes piled high within dishes, compotes stacked upon cake stands, a grape-bordered tray depicting the Last Supper covering up a General Grant memorial plate. Mounds of magnificent examples of daisy and button, thumbprint, bull's eye, the grape, the acorn, and the lion cluttered buffet, cupboards, tables, dressers, and piano, and some were even stuffed away in cardboard cartons that were pushed under the beds and stored in the basement.

My mother, to my horror and shame, accepted old dishes and glasses that neighbors were planning to throw away; she even rescued a blue vase in the shape of a little hand from a stranger's garbage can. She was, in other words, a collector, and all in the name of culture, in the guise of preserving nineteenth-century glassware. The fact that Mrs. Reginald Garson shared Mother's interest in the collection and preservation of old glass, as well as her reading habits, made up somewhat in Mother's eyes for the fact that she played bridge.

The Garsons were away a great deal of the time,

Mrs. Reginald Garson at her bridge clubs or stalking regally about the library selecting fine books to read, and Mr. Garson at his farm, down by Levick's Mill. Little Billy was usually with one or the other of them, or if left at home, he was quiet as a mouse. Too quiet, too mouselike, in a dreadful, maddening way, forever standing and staring and grinning. Any time of the day or evening one of us might look up and see him standing in a doorway or, getting bolder, standing in the same room with us, not talking or making a trace of noise, only grinning his broad, sly little grin. Mother said we were unkind, that the poor little child just wanted a friend.

"Be nice to him when you see him," she urged. "He's sure to be a bright little boy, since his mother's a teacher. And goodness knows, the Garsons have always had brilliant minds."

But after a while we could see that she began to feel jumpy, too, and she uttered a high little squeal of protest one morning when she got up and began to dress and saw, in the mirror, the reflection of little Billy eyeing her smilingly as she tugged at her corset.

Mr. Garson was always bringing us things from his farm, carrots and tomatoes and string beans wrapped up in big brown paper bags or gunny sacks, clumps of earth still clinging to the carrots and other vegetables pulled out of the ground. One day he asked Mother if we drank much milk.

"Oh, yes," Mother answered. "We're a milk-drinking family. The children all love it and I drink it instead of coffee. We stay healthy on milk."

That evening when Mr. Garson came home from the farm he had a huge tin pail of milk in the car. As he carried it into the house the milk splashed against the sides of the bucket and down onto the rugs, but Mr. Garson did not even notice that.

"There you are," he said triumphantly. "You'll stay healthy on milk all right. I'm glad to let you have all you can drink."

When he left and lumbered up the stairs, we all rushed for the milk pail, but Mother stopped us.

"Don't touch it," she hissed. "Don't one of you touch a drop of it."

We looked at her as though she had gone crazy. "Not touch it?" Eloise asked. "But we're all out of milk, and now we can have this for supper."

Mother picked up the pail and set it on the table, looking at it as though there were snakes in it instead of milk.

"It's not pasteurized," she whispered, looking up at the ceiling, as though expecting Mr. Garson to be looking down at her through a hole. "We can't touch it. No telling who milked those cows and how many germs he had on his hands or how many germs there were in the bucket when the milk went into it."

"But all that milk," Helen said, agonized. "What in the world will we ever do with it? You can't throw milk away. If Mr. Garson ever found out—"

"Mr. Garson's not ever going to find out what we do with his milk. As far as he's concerned we drank every drop of it, until we almost burst."

She went out on the back porch where we kept Laddie's dish and brought it in the house. Then, with the soup dipper, she filled the bowl to the brim and set it down on the floor. Laddie came running to his bowl, but he stopped as he came near it, as though he had been lured by a mirage. He got milk sometimes but always in little dabs, leftovers from breakfast or milk turned sour. This was something he could not believe, and he kept away from it as though he knew that if he so much as smelled at it he would be given a cuff on the head for being so presumptuous.

"Go ahead, you stupid dog," Mother said affectionately, pushing his muzzle down into the milk.

And Laddie drank. Drank in long, rapturous laps, looking up every now and then to lick his milky chops and stare beadily at Mother as though he, too, thought she was crazy. Mother refilled his bowl until he could no longer drink, and he finally waddled out of the kitchen, overfed, confused, and delighted.

"Give him the rest of it for breakfast," Mother said. And so there would be no mistake about it, she poured the remainder of the milk into an empty fruit jar which she labeled "Laddie's milk" and put it in the icebox.

The next night Mr. Garson came home with another huge pail of milk, frothy and warm and unpasteurized.

"There's already some left over from last night," Helen said after he had left, pouring a lavish bowlful for Laddie.

"Laddie'll drink it in a day or two," Mother reassured her. "Then we'll be rid of it and Mr. Garson will never be the wiser."

But when Mr. Garson brought a third pail of milk the next night, she began to be worried.

"There are already four jars of milk for Laddie in the ice box," Helen said as she rummaged around in the pantry for another jar. "I think he'll get tired of it if we don't stop giving it to him."

"I'm just dying for a glass of *real* milk," I said thirstily. "Can't we start taking milk again tomorrow or get some at the grocery store?"

For Mr. Garson had been out on the front porch when the milkman came the day before, and he had airily brushed the milkman away.

"I'm feeding them with really good milk now," he had said, "from the best cows in Randolph County. Don't be leaving any more of that bottled whitewash."

"Tomorrow," Mother said, a little harried frown appearing on her forehead, "Mrs. Sears comes to help clean and we'll give her some of it. She'll be glad to get it, with all those children."

"But it's unpasteurized," Eloise protested. "You

said it had germs. Poor Mrs. Sears and her children will get the germs, too."

"She doesn't know it's not pasteurized," Mother snapped illogically. "What she doesn't know won't hurt her."

Mrs. Sears was delighted to get the milk, but Mother made her wrap newspapers around the jars that she took so that none of the Garsons would see she was carrying the milk away. In similar fashion in the past Mother had seen that unwanted gifts of dead squirrels, rabbits, and other repulsive—to us finicky females—foodstuffs given us by well-meaning friends were spirited out of the house in disguise.

"I'd boil this milk first, Mrs. Sears," Mother said, looking guilty.

"Why boil this good milk, Mrs. Elsea?" Mrs. Sears asked, laughing heartily. "It takes the flavor away from milk to boil it."

We already knew that. We had boiled some of the milk ourselves, since Mother was aware that this would kill any bacteria, but none of us, as true milk fanciers, liked the funny taste of home-boiled milk.

"Just a precautionary measure, that's all," Mother said to Mrs. Sears. "It doesn't hurt to boil anything you eat or drink, not a thing."

There were still five jars in the icebox. Suddenly they seemed to multiply like guinea pigs, and where there were five one day, there would be ten the next, with the icebox crammed to overflowing, and jars of milk sitting on top of the box and on the kitchen table, growing sour. Mother let me feed three stray cats, although she hated cats around, but even that didn't make a big loss in the milk supply. And Laddie had gotten so he couldn't even sniff at a bowl of milk. We would drop sugar lumps in it for him or crumple up a piece of bread or place his meat in it. But he would patiently try to seek out every bit of bread and meat and only drink the milk when it was absolutely necessary in order to get the rest of his food.

One night when I came out to the kitchen before going to bed, I saw Mother pouring jars of milk into the sink.

"To throw away food is waste, and waste is sin, and I'll be punished for this," she said angrily, and I could tell she hated that milk and those best cows in Randolph County. "But I'd be punished if you girls drank any of it, so the devil will get me one way or the other."

The milk kept coming in, and Mrs. Reginald Garson kept going out to play bridge almost every night, accompanied reluctantly by a rather grouchy Mr. Garson, who made no secret of the fact that he thought cards were "woman stuff." Sometimes they would leave Billy with one of the neighbors, and later the neighbors would bring him back home and leave him with Mother. Often during the day Mrs. Reginald Garson simply deposited Billy in the children's room of the library, informing Mother she would not even know he was there, he was so good, and then departing. She had earlier told Mother that Billy was a bookish child who already seemed to derive a great pleasure from merely holding her copy of Plato's *Dialogues*, although naturally at the moment it was beyond him. It was true that Billy made no noise at all in the library, but Mother knew he was there when she went into the children's room and found shelf after shelf of books piled on the floor. Billy was building with them as if they were blocks. Doubtless none of them had the color and size of the *Dialogues*.

Mother still told people what a nice family she had in her apartment and what fine minds the Garsons all had, and that Mrs. Reginald Garson read only the best books in the library, but she seemed to leave something unsaid, too.

"Why, he wasn't a bit of trouble," she said to Mrs. Reginald Garson the first time she had taken care of Billy after one of the neighbors brought him back home to her. "Just as quiet as a little mouse."

But the little mouse began to jangle her nerves until, later on, she began to invent lengthy excuses as to why she was not going to be home in the evening. She was going over to Mrs. Cardin's, or she might be detained at the library, or she had promised to go to a missionary meeting. She did not know what to say when Mrs. Reginald Garson kept leaving Billy in the children's room of the library. Billy, even though he was only five years old, was a patron and had every right to be there, and the young were always encouraged to develop the library habit early.

Mother was mindful of the fact that one must not judge little boys in libraries too harshly. Young horrors with dripping noses and wild-looking hair reading *Boys' Life* as they noisily chewed their gum or crunched jawbreakers and shuffled their muddy shoes under the tables might end up some day as college presidents or congressmen. And Mr. Carnegie had written wistfully of picturing the thousands of schoolboys sitting in his libraries and seeing himself a little fellow among them. He probably looked down lovingly now at all the little boys who came skipping, running, jostling, or leaping up the library entry steps, their reading experience in the Moberly library their first push up the ladder of fame and fortune.

Still and all, Billy, not yet a schoolboy, never seemed to realize that books were to be read, or at least, since he was just five, *looked* at, not built with. Even though his mother was a Ph.D. schoolteacher and his grandparents were brilliant, little Billy did not quite understand what books, except Plato, were for. This was possibly because he was only half Garson. The Hoppers, who had contributed to the other half of him, had never been scholars.

The night when I saw Mother closest to crying, she who never wept nor showed a trace of weakness, was when Billy, who had been down in the children's room most of the afternoon, was deposited with her in the evening while the Garsons went off to a bridge party. Eloise and Helen and I had to contribute a large share of our time to watching him or being watched by him, but the responsibility was Mother's.

All of a sudden Billy was nowhere to be seen. He had been sitting on the couch the last time Helen had noticed him, and now he was gone.

"You go find him, Peggy," Helen said. "He's probably outdoors. Make him come in so he won't run away." But Billy wasn't outdoors with any of the children.

"Maybe he's gone upstairs to his own house," Mother suggested, slightly alarmed. "Go look, Helen." And she herself went into our bedroom and kitchen and dining room and even the bathroom, but saw no sight of him.

"He's not upstairs, Mama," Helen said breathlessly. "Everything's all dark and he isn't there."

Each of us was dispatched to a neighbor's house to see if Billy had been there, while Mother looked frantically out in the yard. There was no trace of him anywhere.

"That's what they get," Mother said furiously, "leaving their child with any Tom, Dick, and Harry." And then, blasphemously, "They'd be better off if they weren't so cultured and didn't read as many books and took a little better care of their own family."

We followed her into the house, frightened ourselves, and thinking we would never again tell Billy to go away and quit staring at us if we could only see his dear little red head before us again. Laddie started to go under the couch for an extra nap, and suddenly he gave a dismayed yelp. When I raised up the cover at the end of the couch I saw that curly red head sticking out, the dear little grin on his face broader and slyer than ever. Billy had unpacked one of Mother's cartons of antique china and held a piece of broken blue glass in his hands.

That was when we thought Mother was going to cry. I guess she thought of all those eternal jars of milk out in the kitchen, and she saw Billy lying under the couch like a quiet, unbearable little elf surrounded by pieces of shattered blue antique glass, and she remembered that just this afternoon this same little elf had discovered a new way to play with books—they could be dropped from a library window into the alley. She thought of Mrs. Reginald Garson going out to her endless bridge parties and discussing books and culture and Mr. Garson coming into the house with his unclean buckets of milk. She realized she had not had a decent glass of milk herself for weeks, and she could not see how life would ever straighten itself out.

I suppose Eloise and I were the ones who helped to reorganize life for Mother, although she never knew it, and her problems would have seemed more unsolvable than ever if she had. Eloise and I fought.

Not quiet fights, with both of us sulking in corners and refusing to speak to each other, or even half quiet fights, with one of us shouting and the other sulking and refusing to speak. But we fought with shouts and screams and fists and feet, our anger filling the house and going beyond it.

Not all of the time, of course, and never when Mother was home. As a rule we got along amiably, even banded together, after a fashion, against Helen, who, because she was the oldest, tried to enforce laws by virtue of her age and get us to do the dishes or dust or run errands to the grocery store or carry notes up the alley to her friend Lucille. If Helen told me to do something that I did not want to do, and Eloise did not care about my doing it, I was in luck, because with two persons rebelling against her wishes, Helen finally ended up doing it herself. But if Eloise decided I should do it, I knew I was defeated. I was never defeated, however, until I had fought against it first. Like an old warrior who knew the battle would never be his, I would resist to the end, the end often being a down-on-the-floor fight with Eloise.

What we fought over that particular day was the carrying out of the garbage. Carrying out the garbage was not as easy then as it is today, when I can open the service door, drop the garbage in a can, and never see it again. Mother, the saver of cultural treasure, even saved uncultured refuse – garbage. She had a theory that burying garbage in the garden gave life to the soil, that as the garbage rotted it acted as a fertilizer, as good as manure and cheaper and less offensive. Whoever took the garbage out also took a shovel and dug a hole in the garden and emptied the garbage into it, making a little well of life for the garden. The joker to this practice was that the garden was so full of little wells of life — rotting garbage — that wherever one dug, one struck one of them, and it took a person with the skill of a surveyor and second sight to avoid them.

I would rather do anything in the world than take a paper full of garbage into the garden and hunt for a place to bury it. I envied people with normal mothers who let them throw their garbage sanely into a garbage can at the end of the back porch. Or even people who saved their garbage and fed it to their pigs — watermelon rinds, potato peelings, and all. I think I would rather have had a yard full of pigs to eat garbage than dig those awful graves for it. Even Laddie must have hated it, because every time he tried to dig a hole to bury a bone he unearthed a piece of rotting tomato or moldy bread.

So it was the question "Whose turn is it to bury the garbage today?" that ultimately solved Mother's problem for her. Helen and Eloise had decided it was my time to do it and I had decided it was not; thus, no peace conference could have prevented what Mr. and Mrs. Garson heard. Perhaps Eloise slapped me, or maybe I pinched her. However the fight started, we shouted in anger, we screamed, we punched and slapped, and we were on the floor pounding at each other, shouting, "You're trying to kill me," "I *will* kill you," "I hate you," "I'll knock your head off for that," in the best alley rat technique, more like the high-school boys who fought on vacant lots on the way home from school than Mrs. Carrie Hutton Elsea's dainty little daughters.

When the fight was at its bloodiest and loudest we heard Mr. Garson's booming voice. "Girls, girls, what's going on here!"

Lying on my back, I could see his astonished face as he stood in the doorway, staring as though he were witnessing a murder. Behind him was Mrs. Reginald Garson, looking more cultured and refined than I had ever seen her, but horrified, too, culture and horror making her appear more awesome and unapproachable than I had dreamed it was possible to be.

Eloise got off of my stomach and both of us jumped up, gasping.

"We're playing," Eloise said. "We're only playing."

"We pretend we're mad," I panted. "Every so often we do this."

My stomach felt as though a rock had dropped on it from Eloise sitting on it, and I could see with pleasure and pride that Eloise's right ear was red and fiery looking where I had batted it with my fist a moment before.

"It's a strange way to play," Mr. Garson said gruffly. "You girls could hurt each other if you aren't careful."

Billy appeared in the hallway now, sticking his head around the door to grin at us. His grandmother drew him back sharply and, I think, fearfully, and in another moment the three of them went up the stairs, Mr. Garson still mumbling, "Kill each other if they don't look out."

Eloise and I began to giggle. We giggled silently, holding our hands over our mouths and shaking with delight. We gasped until our sides ached with locked-up laughter, and we got down on the floor and muffled our heads in pillows so that the laughter could come out at last without the Garsons hearing us.

"You girls could hurt each other," Eloise snickered, and this seemed so funny that we rolled deliriously on the floor, snorting and coughing.

Helen came into the living room looking injured and haughty.

"I hope you all are satisfied," she said, eyeing us disdainfully. "*I* buried the garbage."

We could not laugh silently any longer, and we howled with laughter, wonderful, unrestrained, common joy. Laddie began to bark excitedly and nip at our shoes and our clothes, and we encouraged him, lying back on the floor to giggle afresh in the midst of the bedlam.

The Garsons decided to go to Chicago to take Billy to his mother and live there for a while themselves. Mother could bear that. It was not as though they were moving to someone else's apartment because they preferred it to hers. The Garsons had a legitimate excuse for moving — Mother never knew about the fight — and she could drink pasteurized milk again. Life had untied some of its knots.

Mother was surprised to find a stack of cheap mysteries and love stories upstairs that the Garsons had left behind. Mrs. Reginald Garson had even thrown a perfectly good piece of antique glassware in the refuse can, a pickle dish with actress Kate Claxton's picture on it and the motto "Love's Request Is Pickles." All this made Mother wonder if Mrs. Reginald Garson was as cultured as she was supposed to be, in spite of her sophisticated reading preferences. Do you suppose all that checking out of intellectual material from the library was only for show? Was it possible that, like Billy, she only *held* her Plato? It might have been Mr. Garson who read the mysteries — but those *love stories*.

And no one who knew a treasure would discard a Kate Claxton pickle dish.

13

THE CHRISTIAN SOLDIER

For several of my growing-up years, whenever I considered what God probably looked like, I always thought He must resemble Mr. Carnegie. For one thing, both Mr. Carnegie and God, bearded and benign, looked down at me from on high, Mr. Carnegie from the library entry wall, and God from His Heaven. I never doubted that both of them had my well-being at heart, since I tried to please them both. I always looked up respectfully at Mr. Carnegie when I came into the library, and thanked him, whenever I thought about it, for his kindness to Moberly. He was actually more real to me than God.

On the other hand, God and I were certainly not strangers, since I prayed to him nightly, with special prayers in between for emergencies and for extra benefits. Then there were the thank-you prayers for letting me come through the emergencies unscathed, and expressions of gratitude for requests granted. Mother had brought us up to extend our thanks politely and swiftly when people were kind to us.

"Who's going to send you Christmas presents *next* year if you don't show some manners?" she would ask.

Rather than do without both Christmas presents and God's beneficence, I was always lavish with my thank-yous, even though those to God were sometimes given on the run. One could not always stop and go down on one's knees, and surely God could catch the hasty and informal, but nevertheless heartfelt, prayers of thanks sent up to Him while I was rushing home from school — "Thank Thee, God, for letting me pass my arithmetic test" — or hurrying off to a movie — "Thank Thee, that I found the quarter I thought I'd lost."

I had no qualms about involving Him in problems that others might consider beneath His notice, but in spite of my familiarity with Him, I felt the use of "You" was a little disrespectful for one of His authority, and thus always used the more respectful "Thee."

As I neared my teens, I had a running prayer going up to God nightly that someone splendid would fall in love with me soon and let me *know* it. I wanted none of this loved-silently-and-hopelessly-from-a-distance business that I read of in poems and stories, where the hero dare not let his beloved know she is the object of his passion. That was the reason for my two-in-one prayer for the lover who would not only love me but *show* me he adored me.

"And don't let him mind the crooked teeth, please," I often added, slightly embarrassed to seem so petty. All heroines I ever read about had teeth like pearls, but surely not crooked pearls, like mine.

In my heart, however, I did not expect love to be happy. I knew from all my poetry reading that love was pain as well as rapture, and one lived forever after with an anguished heart, or ended up sleeping beside one's lover in a nameless grave in the forest primeval, like Evangeline. In spite of this gloomy knowledge, however, I felt that what was good enough for Evangeline and other doomed heroines was good enough for me.

I often wondered, as I sat on our front porch reading poetry, hidden away by the morning-glory vines and purple and white petunia-filled flower boxes, what I would do if God should speak to me. He had, after all, practically spoken to Edna St. Vincent Millay and the hymn writers, and they had spoken to *Him*, with all of the familiarity of old friends. Edna St. Vincent Millay even laid her finger on God's heart! I certainly wanted to look nice if He did speak to me, so I began to take particular care of my appearance, washing my hair frequently and using vinegar and lemon rinses on it, keeping my fingernails cleaned, and hanging up my clothes instead of dropping them on the floor, so they would not be wrinkled.

I hoped, if God spoke to me, it would be in our garden, not right out on the street where it would be difficult to hear. One of my favorite church hymns had the singer going into a garden when the dew was still on the roses, and God "walks with me and He talks with me and He tells me I am His own." Edna St. Vincent Millay must have been lying on the grass when God spoke to her, and the apostle Paul was on his way to Damascus. There was really no telling—He might even speak to me in the library, since our family Bible was there.

Mother did not think the Bibles in the library were fine enough and had taken our very own Book down, although of course it was put in a special place, and no one could check it out, only look at it. It had been my grandparents' Bible. It was translated out of the original tongues and was four inches thick, and our family records were there. The Bible was full of pictures of such exotic wonders as Herod's Temple, the Molten Calf, and Elijah's altar to the Lord. One year when I needed an angel costume for a Christmas pageant, Mother copied one exactly from a picture in our Holy Bible, and I even carried a scroll in my left hand, like the Bible angel. At the front of the Bible there was a history of manuscript and early printed editions of the Bible, doubtless dictated by God Himself, since the history stated that although the Bible was written by men,

God directed them *what* to write and *how* to write, and warned that a knowledge of the Book was more to be desired than fine gold.

One found marvels there one would never see in the small Bibles that Eloise and Helen and I each owned and always carried every Sunday to Sunday School. Everyone, I presumed, had one's own Bible, just as one had one's own toothbrush. The family Bible, however, was something quite different, extremely holy and sacred, if only because of its size. So, with this special Bible in the library, it was possible God might approach me there.

There were all kinds of holiness *around* the library, too. The Christian Science Church was right next door. My grandmother attended services there, although this seemed almost heretical to me, since we were staunch Methodists. Mother, who had been a Hutton before her marriage, once remarked to Grandmother that she wondered how she could be so contrary, since one branch of the Huttons in England had been best friends of John Wesley, the original Methodist himself. Grandmother only said calmly that *she* was a Crosby, it was Grandpa who had been a Hutton. "I go along with Mary Baker Eddy," she said firmly.

Our, and John Wesley's, church, the Fourth Street Methodist Episcopal Church, South, was in the next block from the library. Another block down on the same street was the Central Christian Church, attended by our cousin Iva Merry. And a couple of blocks to the west of the library was the First Baptist Church, which dunked people when they baptized them, instead of sensibly sprinkling their heads, which surely was just as acceptable to God. Mother strongly disapproved of bodily dunking, and wondered if Baptists did not catch more colds than anyone from such an unhealthy practice.

The Orrs, Mother's grandmother's family, had been Scotch-Irish, and thus Presbyterian, so we were not strangers to that division of Protestantism, whose church was also not too far away from the library.

The Nevinses, next door to us, went to the Catholic Church, two blocks east of the library; thus we had a frame of reference there. Naturally we disapproved of kissing the Pope's toe, but the Catholic practice of not eating meat on Fridays did not bother us at all, since we had salmon croquettes or macaroni and cheese once a week anyway, and Friday was as good a day as any.

Mother had nothing but respect for all of the churches in Moberly, but our God was Methodist and that was that. She hoped Mr. Carnegie had not held it against Methodism as a whole that a well-known Methodist minister of Mr. Carnegie's day — although this was in England — said that Mr. Carnegie was an "anti-Christian phenomenon, a social monstrosity, and a grave political peril." Mother presumed Mr. Carnegie took into account that this was an English and not an American

Methodist speaking. Mr. Carnegie, sharp as a tack, had, in turn, reminded the dissident minister, in an article Mother had in the library, that John Wesley himself had accumulated $250,000 by his writings, and thus was a rich man by the standards of his own time, and would have been as much of an "anti-Christian phenomenon" as he, Mr. Carnegie, was. Mr. Carnegie also pointed out that John Wesley, in his book *The Use of Money*, had advised a man to gain all he could by honest industry and by using the understanding God had given him.

Mother was rather amazed to discover that Andrew Carnegie had been a Swedenborgian in his youth. No offense intended to Mr. Carnegie, of course, and he probably just went along with his father's religion like most children properly did— his mother, of all ridiculous things, leaned toward Unitarianism—but somehow Mother could never imagine Mr. Carnegie holding with those mystical Swedenborgian ideas. You would have thought he'd at least be a Presbyterian, since his parents were Scottish, like great-grandmother Mary Eleanor Orr Hutton from Virginia. Anyhow, he was a good churchgoer in his youth, active in his Sunday School, even teaching in it, and he was also in charge of his Sunday School library. Thus, he would certainly have approved of the fact that his Moberly library was literally surrounded by churches, and that our own Holy Bible was there.

Mother was uneasily aware that Mr. Carnegie,

when he was older, was not as interested in religion as he might have been, but he *did* love to sing hymns, and he approved the free gift to churches of about eight thousand organs, no matter what sect requested one: all Protestant denominations, the Christian Scientists, Swedenborgians, and even Catholics and Jews. Although he himself never gave a whole church away — he did not like all the divisions and sects and conflicting creeds — he believed in other millionaires doing so. He had said so in another famous article he wrote — this also was in the library — called "The Gospel of Wealth." A millionaire should not think how cheaply he could build a church, either, but how perfect it could be made.

Nevertheless, Mr. Carnegie, as well as God, believed in helping those who helped themselves. Once the millionaire gave the fine church building, it was up to the church people to keep it going, just as it was up to Moberly to support the library Mr. Carnegie had given our town. That was just pure common sense, said Mother, and in similar fashion, when I was given a new coat or a dress, it was up to me to keep it neat and clean.

Like Mr. Carnegie in his youth, all members of our family were loyal church and Sunday School goers. We had our own pew, the fourth row from the front, on the left side of the main auditorium, practically under the preacher's nose. We did not really own the pew, of course, and theoretically anyone who got there first could sit in it, but Grandpa had always sat there in what we children thought of as the beginning of time — what he would have thought of Grandmother's defection to Mary Baker Eddy, Mother did not like to think — and so did Mother, and so did her children.

Even Laddie, several times, had sat *under* our pew after following us to church and darting past the ushers. Although the ushers got very excited about this, none of them wanted to be bitten — Laddie was well known to be vicious — so once Laddie was crouched under our pew they pretended they did not know he was there. Laddie must have realized he was in God's house, because he stayed hidden away as quiet as a mouse until the service was over, only licking our legs occasionally and lovingly as we dangled them from the pew. Laddie's being in church was not such a desecration anyway, Mother said. The Pilgrim Fathers, after all, used to bring their dogs to church with them to keep their feet warm.

Although we attended Sunday School on Sunday morning, we usually went to church services in the evening with Mother, since Sunday, which was Mother's one day off from the library, was usually the day she caught up on things at home, such as fixing a balky window, making a blouse for one of her daughters — she knew she would have to rip out the stitches with her nose in Heaven as punishment for sewing on Sunday — preparing a book talk for a school P.T.A. meeting, planning a program for one of her literary clubs, or attending to anything that went wrong with our coal furnace.

The furnace was a monster who lived in our basement. Although he kept us warm in winter, he demanded in return to be fed constantly, relieved of ashes, poked, and just generally watched and humored. Sometimes he made terrible sounds that frightened us and made us run over to Mr. Nevins for help, and sometimes he went out. This was the meanest thing he could do, and he knew it, because it always took a great deal of coal and cajoling to get him started again, and Mother sometimes muttered "H-E-two sticks," which was practically a curse. Anyway, always on Sunday Mother spent some time appeasing him.

By the time Sunday evening arrived, Mother was usually ready to relax with the Lord, and one or all of us girls accompanied her to the service. When I was quite small, I was allowed to go to sleep in church if I wished, my head in Mother's lap, which always felt soft and wonderful because she wore her best Sunday silk dress. Sometimes I was even allowed to take along a book to read, since Mother realized that a sermon was not the easiest thing in the world for a child to understand and endure. Nevertheless, just by being there I was exposed to spiritual uplift that I might remember and profit from.

My most amusing church diversion in summertime was to look at the pictures on the paper fans that were placed in the holders along with the hymnbooks. Without these primitive air conditioners, how else could churchgoers endure the fierce July and August Missouri heat, especially if the unfortunate word "hellfire" was introduced into the sermon? I loved to imagine myself in the places the fan pictures portrayed. My favorite scene was that of Home, Sweet Home, perhaps because it looked so cool, surrounded by vines and roses. I had a room of my own in Home, Sweet Home, hiding behind the vine-shrouded upstairs window shown on the fan. Up there, behind the enchanted window, I lay upon a beautiful canopied bed and drank iced lemonade all day long — possibly being fanned by a servant as I reclined — getting up to play occasionally in the green, tree-shaded yard, but running back whenever I was hot to be cooled, cooled, cooled, by the fan-wielding servant.

My fantasies were obviously inspired by the terrible summer heat suffered in the church pew. People mopped their faces, groaned occasionally from pure misery, and when they stood up for hymn singing their clothes stuck to their skin. As I drowsed and imagined, I finally heard the wonderful words of the preacher, "Now let us pray," which meant the sermon had finally come to an end. This beautiful phrase awakened me immediately and even made me feel cooler. I was ready to sing joyfully "Onward Christian Soldiers," or "The Little

Brown Church in the Dell."

The only trouble about the songs arose when Eloise and I both accompanied Mother to church. Neither Eloise nor I could sing. Eloise had a monotone and I could not reach high notes, so when we tried to sing, our voices sounded so awful to us that we always began to giggle. Mother would glare, but that made the situation funnier still, and often we giggled all through "God the All Terrible King" or "Before Jehovah's Awful Throne." We were especially hilarious when we heard some of the other dreadful voices around us, or noticed the ridiculous way most people looked when they sang, their mouths opening and closing like frogs and fish, and their eyebrows moving up and down.

"You're in the Lord's house," Mother would whisper warningly. She was comforted, however, by knowing that even though we were disgracing her with our laughter, at least we were *there*, which was more than many young people were. Whether we knew it or not, we were momentarily safe in the arms of Jesus.

Usually, all the way home from church, I sang my favorite hymn, "Onward Christian Soldiers," which was rousing, vigorous, and reassuring, full of marching soldiers and waving banners. I marched like a soldier, waving my handkerchief like a banner. "Forward into ba-a-a-tle, see His banners go." Sometimes Eloise sang "Glory! Glory! Hallelujah," from her favorite, "Battle Hymn of the Republic," which was just as rousing, since it was filled with lightning, a swift sword, and a crushed serpent. We always sounded better outdoors than in the church.

Miracles happened fairly frequently in our family, and this, of course, was only natural when a family was as close to the Almighty as ours was. Most of the miracles centered around Laddie, who led a much more active and unfettered life than we, and whose life was thus frequently endangered. Laddie roamed. He was adventurous, amorous, and spirited, and his escapades several times took him to death's door. We were proud that he was a real male, with a penchant for getting into trouble, and he was doubtless proud that we were true females and needed him.

In any event, God also realized we needed Laddie, because He once directed us to the dog pound just as Laddie, who had been picked up by the cruelest creature in the world, the dogcatcher, was about to be exterminated.

When Laddie bit the paper boy, who was the son of the chief of police, Laddie faced almost certain destruction. The paper boy swore Laddie was a mad dog, but we knew Laddie was only frothing at the mouth from rage because the paper boy aimed the paper at *him* when he threw it, instead of at the porch where it belonged. Mother and the Lord handled this crisis quietly.

"Remember, Mr. Ferris, your re-election is coming up soon," she told the paper boy's angry father.

"The girls and I love this little dog and need him for our protection."

Well, chain him up after this, then," grumbled the police chief.

God was always rescuing Laddie from cars that *almost* killed him — one of Laddie's favorite diversions was car-chasing — and once a car ran directly over him, but he crouched close to the street and escaped without a scratch. The true miracle, however, was the time Laddie was at death's door from poison — not everyone in the neighborhood appreciated him as his own family did. This time the Lord must have been trying to teach Laddie a lesson, because here again Laddie was close to dying for a great part of an entire terrible day. It was either the Lord, or Mr. Carnegie, or perhaps both, since this was such a critical danger, who came to the rescue this time, because somebody powerful directed Mother to mention Laddie's peril to the library caretaker, who came out to our house and forced a handful of lard down Laddie's throat. Of course Laddie would have bitten him if he had been strong enough, because the lard made him sick, but it did the trick, and our protector was returned to us.

As librarian, Mother was on good terms with the keepers of all God's houses in Moberly, and often helped them find material they wished to use in their sermons. The only misunderstanding she ever had with any of them was the time one of the local priests announced to her that it was unnecessary for him, since he was God's representative here on earth, to have a library card in order to take out books. As a holy man he could be trusted to return any books he took out, and the insistence upon a card implied that he was dishonest and needed to be checked upon. This announcement embarrassed Mother, who was strongly aware of the importance of good public relations, especially among the clergy. Still, none of the Protestant ministers had demanded exemption from a rule.

"I would not," she informed the father politely, "even allow Mr. Carnegie himself to take out a book unless he had a library card."

She somehow felt as though the Pope of Rome had a hand in this unfair request. And she could have told the priest, although naturally she would not be so rude, of an eighteenth-century cardinal she had read about, the Vatican's own library director, who stole books ruthlessly, not just from libraries but from homes of his friends. He stuffed stolen books under his robes until he looked like a great sausage, puffed up with his pilfered loot. Remembering this story, she could not help looking thoughtfully at the priest as he protested to her about not being trusted, and wondering what some of those bulges were beneath his coat.

One of the Protestant ministers, it is true, complained bitterly about having *Elmer Gantry* on the shelves, but Mother held her ground there, too. Sinclair Lewis was one of the important writers of the time, and like him or lump him, he belonged in a public library. If his book helped some preachers to examine their souls more carefully, it had done some good. Most of the other Protestant ministers simply ignored *Elmer Gantry*, but the book was so popular with lay readers that the board approved the purchase of a second copy.

Exposed as I was to good literature, it was not strange that I wished to produce some of my own. The official Methodist Episcopal Church, South, Sunday School magazine, *The Torchbearer*, published down in Nashville, Tennessee, often accepted poems, articles, and drawings sent into one of their departments, the Sun Parlor, and Mother, who strongly approved of my plan to become an author, suggested I begin with *The Torchbearer*. Andrew Carnegie had published articles in his Sunday School paper, *The Dewdrop*, and then he went out and became a millionaire, although not from his literary work. I was already a fairly experienced writer, since I had composed the eighth grade class poem. I might not be Millay or Teasdale or William Cullen Bryant, but nevertheless I could make words rhyme.

My poem for *The Torchbearer*, however, was composed in free verse, which I considered very modern and daring, perhaps too much so for a church magazine, Mother warned. It was about the quarry, my favorite place in all of Moberly. First, you went to the end of Gilman Road, crawled over a fence, and then you were in Sandison's Pasture, which smelled deliciously of cows and wildflowers and woods. Church and school picnics were held there. You kept on walking until all of a sudden you were on the edge of a cliff, and looked down, down, down, into the quarry filled with water. The quarry was dangerous. It was bottomless, so children believed, and ice skaters and swimmers had drowned in it, but this did not keep ice skaters and swimmers away from it. People died, each individual skater and swimmer realized, but he also knew well that death was only for others; it would not snatch him away.

Mother let me type the final copy of my poem on the library typewriter in the Private Room, slowly, with one finger, the way she herself had learned to type her library reports and records. She also provided me with a used brown manuscript envelope that library materials had been sent in, so that my poem would be sent off in professional fashion. She warned me sensibly that if I were going to become a writer I must expect disappointments and rejections, even though I could write like Shakespeare. Not all editors used good judgment.

I almost forgot my concern about God speaking to me, what with all the excitement of writing poetry and waiting to hear from *The Torchbearer*. One afternoon when I came into the library after school, Mother beckoned me immediately into the Private Room.

"Well, some editor showed common sense, after all," she said, handing me a letter—naturally she had opened it, since it was from *The Torchbearer*. It was not a real letter at all; it was only a printed form, but the name of my poem, "The Quarry," had been inserted after the words "*The Torchbearer* is pleased to announce acceptance of your poem. . . ."

I stared at the letter and then at Mother, in wonder, and saw that there were tears in her eyes, although she was smiling proudly. And then and there God spoke to me, right in the library. It was not a *real* voice, of course, like a person's, but it made me feel as though a whole spring day or a Christmas morning had been poured inside of me. I knew whose voice it was, all right, just as surely as Edna St. Vincent Millay or the hymn writers knew when God spoke to them. I wanted to leap and shout, and run outdoors and push the grass apart and lay my finger on God's heart, or march down Main Street like a Christian Soldier, singing "See His banners go!" All I said, though, was "gee," and I am not sure whether I said it to Mother or God.

Later on, when I had time to think about it all calmly, and separate the excitement of God's speaking to me from the wonder of *The Torchbearer's* acceptance of my poem, I realized I was glad God had spoken the way He did, not a real sound at all. This was so special, so personal, that I would not have wanted even Mother or Mr. Carnegie to hear Him.

14
THE QUEEN OF SONG AND DANCE

Few persons in Moberly ever utilized the volumes on genealogy that were available in the library with the diligence and eagerness that Mrs. Wilbur brought to her researches. Not that Moberly folk were uninterested in their ancestors—there were local chapters of both D.A.R. and U.D.C.—but a great many residents were descended from families who had lived in the area or nearby counties for enough generations to know who their grandfathers or great-grandfathers had been and where they came from. Mother's own father had been one of the early settlers in Moberly when it was a new town after the Civil War. She was a member of the United Daughters of Confederacy, and her great-great-grandfather Hutton had fought in the Revolutionary War when the family still lived down in Virginia. Before *that*, members of her family had lived in England, and one of the Crosbys had been a

Sir.

This greatly impressed Mrs. Wilbur, who did not even know where her grandfather had come from, let alone her great-great. Although this seemed inconceivable to Mother, who was family conscious, she used to comfort Mrs. Wilbur by reminding her that Mr. Wilbur was a Mason, and she could be proud she was married to him; that was honor enough for any woman.

Mother had a preference for Masons. Father had been a Mason, and so had Grandpa and his father before him. We had all sorts of Masonic relics wrapped up in tissue and brown paper on the top shelf in the closet: Father's sword, his Masonic fez and uniform. In the black metal box with her Valuables — her pearl brooch in the chamois bag, her gold Swiss watch, a wide-banded gold wedding ring, and the pearl earrings Grandpa had brought her from New Orleans when she was a girl — were more Masonic symbols. Father's Knight Templar charm, with its crown and cross and mystic letters, was there, as well as a stickpin with more mysterious letters on it, and a huge black and gold ring, any of which had strange and wonderful powers when shown to a Mason, particularly if one were in trouble. If anyone doubted this, Mother could back up her faith with a vivid story of the time when she was a girl and had taken a train trip by herself.

"Two loud men kept looking at me," she would say, "and making remarks. There was whiskey on their breath." She would pause dramatically. "Then all of a sudden I took out Papa's Knight Templar charm and held it out toward them. They drew back as if I'd handed them a snake, and got real white. Then all the rest of the trip they couldn't do enough for me."

"And besides," she often added, "if we're ever old and destitute we can always go to a Masonic Home and be taken care of."

So life really had no terrors for us. The Masons, fezzed and ornamented with powerful charms, would always provide.

The fact that Mr. Wilbur was a Mason made him and Mrs. Wilbur immediately eligible as tenants when they came to look at our upstairs apartment for rent. Mr. Wilbur was a rather quiet, shy-looking man who sold flour. Mrs. Wilbur was large and jolly, and delighted at the thought of having a librarian for a landlady. They were nice substantial folk, Mr. and Mrs. Wilbur, and Mother was pleased to have them as tenants.

I could not be bothered about such mundane things as tenants, however, not even if a king and queen should happen to move upstairs, because I, at this time, was of all importance to myself. I was growing up. I suddenly realized that I was a person, I was the world. I had freckles. That was an agony more terrible, more shattering, than the fact that men had fought and died a few years before and more would fight and die in a few years to come.

But I had black eyelashes and eyebrows that would never have to be dyed, and I had heard someone say about me, "Those lovely eyes." That was more important, more wonderful, than Lindbergh's flight across the Atlantic. What did it matter that the Wilburs were bringing peace and substantial respectability to our house after a succession of undesirable renters, when I had been promised a jar of Stillman's freckle cream if I made an A in arithmetic?

"Although it will burn your skin off," Mother promised grimly. "Better to have those few little freckles than no skin at all."

Mother was opposed to creams and newfangled beauty methods. But what could she do with a daughter who looked in the mirror and wept and shouted that her life was ruined, she might as well die, because she had freckles and straight hair.

My chest was beginning to swell. Where all of my life I had been flat, suddenly my bosom began to ripple uncertainly, achingly. My friend Annabel and I discussed the phenomenon.

"Everybody gets a bosom," Annabel said, with superiority. "Margaret, Bernice, everybody."

"I don't want one," I decided.

"If you don't have, you'll never be grown-up, and no one will ever want to marry you or kiss you." Annabel was condescending.

"Why won't they? What difference will that make?"

"I don't know." Annabel looked uncertain. "But they won't, anyway."

"Where does it come from, the bosom?" I asked, puzzled.

"It just grows, like anything grows," Annabel floundered. "Someday you'll be as big in front as — as Mrs. Wilbur who lives at your house."

I recalled Mrs. Wilbur's huge, pendulous bosom that pushed ahead of her body, and I shuddered.

"I shan't either be like Mrs. Wilbur."

Annabel giggled. "Yes, you will. Just exactly."

It was amazing to think about that. I looked down wonderingly at my thin body. Supposing I did start to grow big like Mrs. Wilbur. I would look just the same as I did now except for my chest, which would billow roundly in front of me; it would weigh me down, I would be forever about to fall on my face. It was an unbearable thought.

From this time on Mrs. Wilbur's bosom fascinated me. It was impossible for me to take my eyes off of it whenever I saw her. It was so definitely a part of Mrs. Wilbur. Whereas my chest was inconsequential and small, hardly to be noticed, Mrs. Wilbur's seemed the most important thing about her. It surged before her, large, protruding, immense. It seemed as though it were Mrs. Wilbur's bosom that went places, and Mrs. Wilbur, attached to it, merely followed.

One Saturday morning when I had gone upstairs to give Mrs. Wilbur a telephone message that had come for her while she was at the grocery store, she invited me to sit down. She was wearing a pink kimono wrapped loosely about her, and she looked warm and pretty. Mrs. Wilbur wasn't young, but she wasn't old, either, and she was fun to talk to: she always had plenty to say. She was working on some sort of costume for her church program, a piece of yellow cloth folded in her lap.

"Let me hold this against you," she said, getting up. "It's for a tiny little woman who's no bigger than you are. I can get an idea from you."

As she held the costume up to me the folds of her kimono opened at her throat, and all of a sudden I thought I would scream. I was filled with fear, with a wild horror, and all I wanted to do was to get away from Mrs. Wilbur, from her room, from a newly discovered terror.

"Mama's calling me, I think," I muttered incoherently, and I rushed from the room, while Mrs. Wilbur stared at me as though I had gone crazy.

I did not want to see anyone. I ran out of the house and fled to my refuge, the little grove in the empty lot, and crawled into my bush cave, panting. Margaret came by and I heard her calling me. We were going to play tennis, but I did not want to see Margaret. I had to think, to figure things out. Because I had seen a terrible spectacle. Mrs. Wilbur's bosom was not white like her neck and arms; it was all colors, red and blue and green, in awful designs. This, then, was a bosom; this is what I must have to be grown up, to be married, to be kissed, to be like Margaret, Bernice, everybody in all the world.

I shuddered, crouching flat and miserable on the slanting floor of the cave. Where had the designs come from? Wherever the bosoms had come from, I supposed. Annabel said they just grew like anything else. But what made the colors and the designs, blue anchors and bright red hearts, and the green snake winding itself over and around them? I didn't want a green snake on my body, I didn't want any bosoms at all, ever, if they were going to come all colors. Not even if Annabel and Margaret and Mildred, everybody, had them.

Then suddenly I remembered something. Everybody didn't have designs. There were the ladies I had seen in pictures in the art book, and women I had watched nursing their babies, and even Mother herself once or twice when she was dressing. They were all one color; they didn't look as though there hadn't been enough skin and God had patched them up with a remnant that didn't match. But how could you tell how you were going to turn out, like the ladies in the art book, or Mrs. Wilbur? Maybe it was like freckles, some people had them and some people didn't. But I wanted my bosom to be white when it came, I wanted it to be white!

I knew now why Mrs. Wilbur always wore high necks. I would wear high-necked dresses, too, if my bosoms grew with designs. I would not want anyone ever to know about it. I would have to wear high-necked dresses all the time, even in the middle of summer, and I could never wear a bathing suit. I could never have any fun in all my life again.

I began to cry, feeling sorry for myself and even for Mrs. Wilbur, although I somehow held her responsible for all this misery. This, then, was growing up, finding out horrors such as those I had discovered this morning. Because supposing I was one of those people, like Mrs. Wilbur, who had designs. I looked down at my little unwanted bosoms fiercely, hating them, hating all of life.

The next few days were like a terrible dream, and I suffered so many stomachaches and crying spells that Mother thought I might have a bad appendix. If the designs came, how would they come? Would I wake some morning and they would be there, like the time when I had measles? Or would they come all of a sudden sometime when I was at a party, and show above the neck of my dress? Or would they come one at a time, so I would be able to get used to them? And who and what determined what the designs would be? Would they be hearts and anchors like Mrs. Wilbur's were, or strawberries, perhaps, like Martha Finley's birthmark on her arm? I wanted to tell Annabel, to share the secret of my knowledge with her, but I did not dare discuss this shameful thing. And certainly I could not tell Mother, nor Helen, nor Eloise. They would think I was a monster. I would have to endure my unhappiness by myself.

One morning when I woke up there was a red spot at the base of my throat, a tiny welt. This is it, I thought miserably, the designs are coming. I am going to be like Mrs. Wilbur after all and not like the ladies in the art book. I knew that I had expected them to come, they were somehow tangled up in my mind with freckles. Mrs. Wilbur had freckles and she had the designs, so probably everyone with freckles had designs; they were possibly only a more hideous and malevolent branch of the freckle family.

I examined the tiny welt carefully, even borrowing Eloise's magnifying mirror so I could see better. It looked like a mosquito bite, lumpy and inflamed. Maybe it *was* just a mosquito bite, I thought hopefully. Oh, let it be a mosquito bite, I prayed feverishly, staring into the mirror; oh, God, let it be a mosquito bite and not a design, not a heart or an anchor or a snake coming!

The bump grew larger, almost as I watched, a rosy plump knob. A strawberry, I thought in anguish; it is to be a strawberry design. But nothing further happened to the welt. It remained the same size, the same shape, the same color. I looked at it for an hour as I lay across the bed, hating what I saw, but curious, too, wanting to know how the designs came if I was to be spotted with them.

When I finally went into the kitchen for breakfast, I saw Mrs. Wilbur standing outdoors at the vegetable wagon, and I felt a horrible kinship with her. She was wearing her pink wrapper and her bedroom slippers, because it was still early morning. As I peered at her through the window she bought a handful of carrots and a bunch of rhubarb and came on into the house.

"I owe Mrs. Wilbur an egg and she might need it for breakfast," Mother said, as she heard Mrs. Wilbur go up the stairs, and she picked up an egg from our basket of them and went upstairs, following Mrs. Wilbur.

A few minutes later, while I was eating my breakfast and surreptitiously feeling the new lump on my throat, Mother came down the stairs, pale and trembling.

"Good heavens, Carrie, have you had a spell?" Grandmother asked, rushing over to her.

Mother didn't say anything for a minute, just sat down on the day bed, breathing heavily, with a look of amazement in her eyes.

"My God, Mama," she whispered after she had gotten her breath, "there were green snakes climbing all over them, and red hearts, and even a rope with anchors."

Grandmother turned pale now, too. She shook Mother by the arm.

"Carrie, you've lost your mind! Oh, good Lord, the child has lost her mind!"

"I haven't lost my mind, no such thing," Mother replied crossly, shaking Grandmother's hand from her arm. "I'm telling you, I saw this with my own eyes. Her bust—" she paused—"*tattooed*."

Grandmother clutched her own withered little bosoms.

"You mean—"

"Mrs. Wilbur," Mother answered. "She's got both of her bosoms tattooed all over, solid."

"But Mr. Wilbur's a Mason," Grandmother said illogically, as though this fact alone, for some reason, made such a thing as Mother had told her automatically impossible.

"Mason or no Mason, I saw them," Mother insisted. "Saw them with my own eyes. I went up to give her the egg we borrowed from her last night. She was in her slip, no dress on or kimono, and all of a sudden the strap on her slip broke while we were talking."

Tattoo, I knew what tattoo was. Harold Meffert's uncle in the Navy had a flag and a lady tattooed on his arm. Harold said they punched his arm with needles and pushed ink in the holes. Then was that—could it be—

"Then they didn't grow on her?" I cried out. "They were put on with needles, they didn't come of their own accord?"

Mother stared at me as if it were I, now, out of my mind.

"How could a thing like that grow?" she asked. "I never saw such a thing on man or beast before in all of my life. God has too good taste to put anything like that on a person."

"How did you know about them?" she asked, after a moment, suddenly actually aware of me.

"I saw them, too, the other day," I said, blushing.

"Why didn't you tell me?" Mother said wildly. "Why in the world didn't you let me know?"

But I was not paying any attention to her. I was feeling the mosquito bite at the base of my throat, scratching it rapturously, unworried about tomorrow or the next day or all of life to come.

"What do you suppose she used to be?" Mother whispered cautiously to Grandmother, "with *That*?"

"A carnival woman, I'd say," Grandmother answered, looking around the room to be sure Mrs. Wilbur wasn't listening. "A show woman," and as an afterthought, "low shows."

"She's to serve pie tonight at the Beauceant supper," Mother said, trying desperately to merge the Mrs. Wilbur of low shows with the Mrs. Wilbur of the Beauceant pie supper.

"We've had light women and wife chokers," Mother recalled bitterly of some of our previous renters, "and now this. The Lord is doing His best to try me." She got up slowly. "I don't know how to tell her they'll have to leave."

"They've been good, decent people while they've been *here*," Grandmother said quickly.

"That's not the point," and Mother turned the whole problem over in her churning mind. "I've got three young girls growing up, Peggy here, and

Helen, and Eloise. I can't have a woman like that giving them ideas."

She went up the stairs again, this time reluctantly, no egg in her hand. I followed at a discreet distance, although I did not go into Mrs. Wilbur's apartment after Mother, but waited at the top of the stairs, peering over the banister. Now that I knew Mrs. Wilbur's designs were man-made, not God-sent, I wanted to see them again. I regarded them as amazing, marvelous decorations, and Mrs. Wilbur as a fascinating woman from the carnival, the wonderful, glittering shows that came to Moberly every summer.

Mrs. Wilbur was crying. I heard her anguished, hiccuping sobs when I got to the top of the steps, and when I peeked over the banister I could see her lying on the day bed, her face muffled in a pillow. When Mother knocked, Mrs. Wilbur called out between her hiccups, and Mother went uncertainly into the living room.

Suddenly Mrs. Wilbur got up from the bed and snatched at a heavy white piece of cloth that looked like two immense bags and shook it before her, angrily.

"If I'd only worn this steady no one would ever have known. I got to thinking I was so safe. And now by tonight everybody in Eastern Star will know I'm tattooed." She crumpled the huge brassiere up in her hands, staring at it bitterly.

Mother drew herself up haughtily. "Nobody

knows but me, Mrs. Wilbur, and I'm no tale bearer."

"I bet you think I'm a fine person," Mrs. Wilbur said. She blew her nose and struggled to get her hair out of her eyes.

Mother didn't say anything. She, who usually was never at a loss for words, seemed to be overcome by the events of the last half hour.

"I'm a different woman now than I was, Mrs. Elsea," Mrs. Wilbur said, finally. "And I've come a long way."

She stared before her, perhaps at a rough wooden stage with a garish canvas backdrop painted with barelegged girls. (*Step up, folks, the next show starts in ten minutes. Men, get your tickets here, see the tattooed queen of song and dance.*")

"I thought they were beautiful at the time," Mrs. Wilbur went on slowly. "'One for my boy friend in the Navy, one for my beau in the Army,' I told the tattoo man. Old Jim Burns, he was, from my home town. It would turn your stomach to see him. He's got a dotted line across his throat, and underneath it it says 'Cut here.' I wouldn't have gone to a stranger, though. My girl friend got cold feet, all she had was a ship on her shoulder. But I had to have the whole works."

She was silent for a few moments, and Mother was silent, too.

"I never did see either boy friend again," Mrs. Wilbur broke the quietness. "One married some girl in California, never did come back home again, and I don't know what happened to the other. Then I met Joe. And he's such a good man and so respectable. That's one of the reasons I've been trying so hard to find ancestors, so I can be worthy of Joe."

Her voice trembled. She straightened out the huge white brassiere, giving each of the curves a careful punch.

"But if anyone ever found out. . . ." She looked at Mother, her light blue eyes fearful and ashamed.

Mother fingered a Masonic pin of Father's that she was wearing at her neck.

"A Mason sticks by a Mason," she said finally. And you could tell that Mother knew now what gave the Masonic emblems a strange and wonderful power.

The Wilburs lived with us for another year, a year of peace and regular rent payments and almost daily offerings of cake or cookies or pie from Mrs. Wilbur. Even Laddie knew that her step on the stair meant a choice little bone for him or interesting table scraps. It was a year in which I got a jar of freckle cream, and my skin didn't come off as Mother said it would, and neither did the freckles.

When the Wilburs moved, it seemed as though a part of our family was leaving.

"We hate to do you this way," Mrs. Wilbur told Mother apologetically, "but we want a home of our own. We've found a brick house, a five-room bungalow, and Joe thinks now's the time to buy."

The Wilburs still stopped in to visit from time to

time, however, and the *Moberly Monitor-Index* kept us informed of the club meetings and church affairs that Mrs. Wilbur attended. Mrs. Wilbur had by this time exhausted all of the genealogy books in the library without locating an ancestor, but Mother had directed her to the Missouri Historical Society Library in Columbia and had even advised that she hire a genealogical researcher to make things go more quickly. Mr. Wilbur patiently drove Mrs. Wilbur back and forth to the Historical Library so that she could pursue her researches, and he did not seem to mind the money she expended on a private researcher.

One evening when I was working in the library on a theme for my high-school English class, Mrs. Wilbur came running breathlessly into the building.

"I've found my ancestors," she cried out to Mother, "Oh, Mrs. Elsea, I've found them! Some of them came from Virginia, like your folks did. And one of them was a *preacher*!"

She showed Mother a letter she had received from her genealogical researcher, her hands trembling so that Mother could scarcely read the words. She and Mother were so overjoyed that neither of them bothered to whisper. "She thinks one of them fought in the Revolutionary War. I might even get to be a D.A.R.—anyway, for sure a U.D.C. Look, here's a Thaddeus Green in the Civil War! And I came from *him*!"

She was almost dancing with joy, and suddenly

a fantastic tune hummed through my head, and I saw again a picture I had seen when I was twelve, a rough wooden stage filled with barelegged dancing girls in shabby spangled costumes. "*See the tattooed queen of song and dance.*" I heard the shrill, piercing carnival calliope sounding across a dusty field on the edge of town, a field transformed for a few nights into a shoddy glitter of side shows and gambling booths piled high with Kewpie doll prizes. I smelled peanuts and tobacco and dirty clothes and cheap perfume.

"Men, get your tickets here!"

But it was not a tattooed queen of song and dance who stood before us in the library, radiant and laughing, her great bosom heaving with excitement. Underneath the correct pink voile of her dress, the blue anchors and red hearts and green snakes rose and fell with each lift of bosom, and must have been a weird contortion, writhing, twisting in emotion. But they were hidden by pink voile, by the present, by the newly found ancestors from Virginia; they were the forgotten past. No one but a flour salesman, and the town librarian and her mother, and a girl with freckles knew of the strange patterning etched beneath the voile breast of the descendant of Thaddeus Green, Civil War veteran — these four, and some tattoo artist who surely has never forgotten his most amazing work of art.

"'Both of them, each for a boy friend,' she tells me," he must sometimes have recalled to himself, almost unbelieving. "A beautiful job I done, the finest inks, the best designs."

I could see him finger the dotted line about his throat, and the words "Cut here," beneath it, as he meditated. "That's a job won't come off to her dying day."

But the tattoo man was wrong. I think the job came off that night for Mrs. Wilbur as she stood triumphant and magnificent in her hour of glory in the library, showing her line of ancestry to Mother. Her bosoms were at last white and unmarred; they were miraculously cleansed of their impurities, each knot of rope, each curve of snake, each point of anchor, each ruby heart, dissolved forever.

BLOOMERS AND BOY SCOUTS

I am not at all sure that Mr. Carnegie would have approved of one of his librarians losing her bloomers in front of the Central Christian Church, even if it was her extra pair. He saw a lot of sights in his network of libraries, which he surely visited in ghostly guise after his death. (He had, after all, spent a fortune on those buildings and must have wanted to see how things were being run.) Surely none of the sights he encountered on such visits were more strange than that of one of his very proper ladies anxiously asking an embarrassed little girl about eleven or twelve years old, "Did you find them?"

The little girl dug reluctantly in her coat pocket, pulled out a mass of crumpled pink silk, handed it ungraciously to her mother, and burst out crying. Mr. Carnegie, being kindly, would possibly have liked to comfort the little girl — she had lumps on

247

her legs which he, an old-fashioned man himself, knew were caused by the folds of her long underwear. Having many libraries to watch over, Mr. Carnegie probably soon forgot the affair of the lost bloomers. The little girl never for a moment worried about what Mr. Carnegie saw. But she did agonize about Mr. Hilton and the Boy Scouts.

I am sure that Mr. Hilton had some very impressive title, since he was an executive of the National Scout Organization, but to this day all I know is that he dressed in Boy Scout suits, and in the summertime wore khaki shorts. This horrified Mother, because Mr. Hilton was a huge man, broad and tall and hairy, and she never looked directly at him while he wore his shorts. Mr. Hilton had an office in one of the basement rooms of the library building, and he appreciated Mother because she helped him find important information for surveys upon which he was engaged. She approved of him because he was always encouraging the Boy Scouts to come to the library and read, sometimes even herding little groups in himself.

Mr. Hilton felt sorry for our family — I suppose this was because Mother was a widow and we had no manly protection except Laddie — and being a Boy Scout, he tried to do everything he could to give us advantages. Mr. Hilton traveled a lot over the county, and he felt sure that my sisters and I, since our family did not have a car, would enjoy seeing the county, too. He would snatch us from whatever we were doing to take us with him on uninteresting jaunts to Renick and Clark and Huntsville, places we had not the slightest desire to visit, because they were tiny, "one horse" towns near Moberly. But to Mr. Hilton it was as though he were taking us to Chicago or New York or Seattle.

That was just a small misery to be endured. It could be borne, the dull drives over the rutted roads, peering at one small Main Street after another, and being left to sit alone in the parked automobile to stare sleepily at the feed mills and general stores and dusty Fords while Mr. Hilton attended to his business.

But Mr. Hilton's fatherly interest reached its peak when he decided that I should go to the Boy Scout party. All the troops in town were giving it and asking girls, and the women of the Central Christian Church would serve refreshments. When Mother told Mr. Hilton I was not going, he looked troubled.

"She'll be asked," he said finally, looking thoughtful. "She'll get to go."

That night when the telephone rang, Mother answered it.

"It's for you, Peggy," she said, surprised. "Someone wants to talk to you."

"This is Chester's mother," the voice said when I answered the phone. "Chester wants to take you to the Boy Scout party."

I turned around to Mother, bewildered.

"What is it?" Mother was whispering. "What do they want?"

"It's Chester's mother. She says Chester wants to take me to the party."

"Tell her Yes," Mother whispered. "Tell her you'll be glad to go."

"I don't want to go with Chester," I whispered back. "I don't like Chester."

Mother took the receiver herself, and she and Mrs. Wiley had a long pleasant talk, Mother accepting the invitation graciously for me, and at the end giving Mrs. Wiley her favorite recipe for devil's food cake, which Mrs. Wiley wanted to try for the Boy Scout party.

"I don't want to go with him," I protested stormily when Mother came away from the phone. "He has funny ears."

"Don't talk that way," Mother said. "You'd hurt Mr. Hilton's feelings. Chester might not have asked you if Mr. Hilton hadn't told Mrs. Wiley you weren't invited."

I felt awful inside. I had not really been asked as all my friends had been. I had been asked by a mother, and Chester probably did not want to go with me any more than I wanted to go with him. And all on account of Mr. Hilton. I would never be able to hold up my head again. I was disgraced for life.

By the night of the party I felt much happier, and no longer hated Mr. Hilton. I had a new blue dress with tan silk embroidery on the pockets and collar, and I had a shingle, which was a fashionable new hair style with a shaven effect in back, like a boy's, the hair in front brought around in a weak curl. When Mother laid out a clean suit of long underwear for me to put on I was appalled.

"I can't wear long underwear to a party," I shrilled, and I had visions of myself walking around with my long white underwear coming down below my elbows, far below the beautiful blue, short-sleeved dress.

"You'll certainly not go to a party or anyplace without it," Mother said. "A party's as cold a place as home is, or school. You'd take your death of cold."

"But a party," I wailed, distracted. "Everyone will laugh at me."

Mother was one of the last believers in long underwear. Many winters after everyone else had laid it aside, the Elseas were still wearing it, Mother proudly and defiantly, Eloise and Helen and I shamed and tearfully, always aware of the telltale lumps at our ankles and wrists where the underwear stopped and was folded over. The year Mother let us wear long black bloomers with nothing under them was one of the important years of our lives.

Mother had first faced an underwear crisis the year Eloise was a rose in the school operetta. Eloise's teacher had been horrified when Eloise appeared the night of the operetta with her long underwear trailing down her legs under her cheesecloth rose petals. The teacher and Mother had had a quarrel about it backstage, the teacher saying Eloise could not dance with her underwear showing, it wasn't decent, and Mother saying decent people didn't go anywhere without it. Eloise had screamed and carried on so right in front of everybody that Mother compromised and hid most of the underwear up under the rose petals.

In like manner, Mother now skillfully pushed the underwear arms up under the short sleeves of my dress, giving a bunched and padded effect that must have been horrible, but Mother and I both were pleased at the result. After debating with herself several minutes, Mother made another concession to my social life. She rolled the legs of the underwear up to my knees.

"There now, if you take cold you've just yourself to blame," she said, looking worriedly at my legs, which she already could see freezing.

I felt exhilarated and wonderful. My legs and arms were like anyone else's now. I was going to a party. I had a date. The world had opened its heart to me. When Mr. Hilton stopped by to see how I looked, I even felt myself to be in love with *him*.

I put on my hat and coat so I would be all ready when Chester came. When the doorbell rang I ran nervously to the door. Chester was standing silently on the porch, and I went out just as silently and joined him. Chester in school was someone I could yell at or laugh with or help with problems, but being with Chester alone, going to a party, was something different. What did one say to a boy when one went to a party with him; how could I break the terrible silence between us? Chester on his side of the walk, and I on the other side, moved silently through the darkness down Fourth Street, I in an agony of unsaid sentences and laughter which, if they could have gone any further than my mind, I knew would make Chester look at me and see me as I really was, not twelve years old, speechless, and afraid my long underwear would roll down, but a woman in a new blue silk dress, beautiful, interesting, and with practically bare legs.

"I'll see ya," Chester muttered as we reached the Christian Church basement, and he ran over to join a group of boys by the piano, while I went to the middle of the room where my girl friends were standing together giggling.

Mr. Hilton was moving about the room in gigantic splendor. When he saw me he laughed with pleasure and roared across the room, "Here's your girl, Chester, the prettiest girl in the room." I bowed my head in unbelievable embarrassment and shame and saw Chester duck under the coat rack and out of sight. I tried not to let Mr. Hilton see me the remainder of the evening, or Chester, either, and that was not so difficult to do because most of the girls played games together and the boys played their own games. Chester and I did sit together for refreshments, but we did not have to talk, only eat the ice cream and cake and candy and drink cocoa. And we laughed at the speeches made by the senior scouts as though they were the funniest things in the world.

After the party Chester was waiting for me at the door, and again we started down Fourth Street, in silence, as we had come. Just as we got to the house, Chester spoke, his voice sounding loud and harsh in the darkness.

"That sure was funny about the lobsters, wasn't it?"

The lobsters, the lobsters? My mind raced frantically back to the party. There hadn't been lobsters, only the cake and ice cream and cocoa and those pink and green mints. What in the world was he talking about? What should I say: "Yes, it was awfully funny," and laugh, or should I ask him, "What lobsters?"

"Old Ray sure knows how to make a speech," Chester said. "Old Ray's swell."

Old Ray, old Ray. Oh, he meant Ray Harmon, that big Boy Scout who made the long speech. Lobsters, lobsters. He'd told a joke about lobsters. I remembered, I remembered! I hadn't quite heard the ending, but everyone had laughed and I had, too. So I laughed again now, laughed as though I could never quit laughing, and Chester began to laugh, too.

"It sure was funny," I said finally, between gulps

of laughter, and I wished I knew what the lobster joke really was all about. "Well, good night, Chester, I had an awful good time."

"I'll see ya," Chester said, and he jumped from the top step onto the ground, and ran whistling down the street.

"Did your legs get cold?" Mother asked me the minute I came into the house. Who would think of such a thing as cold legs except a mother? All I cared about now in all the world was the wonderful, witty Chester. I had made it home just in time, however. The rolled-up long underwear fell down one leg as I came in the door and dropped down the other leg before I had finished telling Mother about the Boy Scout party.

Mother believed in the importance of warmth in relationship to health. In wintertime warmth to her meant as many clothes as possible, covering as large an area as possible, and an important and voluminous part of warmth was bloomers. My first awful experience with them began when I was in the third grade, and Mother appeared suddenly at school one morning, with a package wrapped in brown paper in her hand. After a brief whispered consultation with my teacher, and a significant patting of the brown paper parcel, Mother beckoned to me to follow her out of the room.

"You forgot your bloomers," Mother whispered, when we got out in the hall. "I nearly went crazy when I saw them lying on your bed, and you out in the cold with nothing on your legs."

Nothing, of course, but a heavy ghostly suit of long underwear, covered with thick black stockings.

"You didn't *bring* my bloomers with you!" I whispered, horrified, knowing only too well that the ugly brown paper parcel held those hideous things that I had forgotten.

"I certainly did. And Miss Payne says we can go downstairs in the washroom and put them on."

This was almost too shameful, too horrible to bear. Down we went to the washroom, into a sheltered cubicle, and the bloomers, black sateen trimmed with ruffles, were transferred from the paper sack onto my rebellious legs.

"You would have frozen," Mother said, jamming the brown paper into her purse. "If I hadn't happened to find those bloomers lying on your bed and brought them over here this morning, you would have been a chunk of ice before the day was over."

But I would gladly have been a chunk of ice or a clod of dirt rather than have anyone in my room know what Mother had come to school for.

"What did she want? Why'd you have to go out of the room?" my seatmate asked.

The little girl behind me poked me in the back. "Did you have to take some medicine? You're crying."

"My aunt died," I said. "That's what she wanted to tell me. My aunt was a princess and lived in St. Louis in a castle. And she died. A beast ate her."

This was wonderful. I remembered all the fairy stories I had read. I could go on and on with this story. But Miss Payne called me to the blackboard to do an addition problem.

"Your bloomer ruffle's showing," my seatmate whispered as I sat down. "It shows this much," and she held her fingers wide, and giggled.

Mother made our bloomers herself, black sateen ones for everyday, pink sateen for best, good firm elastic at the waist, good firm elastic at the knee, and a ruffle jutting out at the knee. She wore them, too, exactly like ours, and every night a row of black or pink bloomers in graduated sizes hung up to dry on the rope clothesline in the basement. I was still wearing sateen the year of the Boy Scout party, but Helen and Eloise, who were practically grown up, were wearing silk, as Mother was. Bloomers, still, to be sure, but silk ones. Helen even had a pair of step-ins, pink georgette with hand-painted flowers on them, that Mother had made her for her high-school graduation, and to take away to college, "just to show the girls," Mother had admonished. "But if you ever wear them, be sure and wear them *over* your bloomers."

A few years later, when I was in college, Mother was still worrying about my bloomers. Her letters to me showed her constant fear that I was not warm enough. "Peggy, for heaven's sake, wear long bloomers and don't have any *bare* space on your legs." Or, "Have you bloomers to wear these cold days? You must not expose your body." Still again, "I noticed you did not have your bloomers on when you were home and I so wish you'd wear them till the cold weather is over, but you *can't change.*"

It was difficult for Mother to understand our objection to bloomers. She herself thought nothing of wearing two pairs of the hated things in very cold weather, or of carrying an extra pair with her when she went out, to be put on in case it turned colder than she thought. For some reason she did not insist that we do this. We carried the rubbers, umbrellas, scarves, and hats that she insisted upon — although we never used them — but I think she realized that if she ever mentioned the carrying of an extra pair of bloomers to us, we would alienate ourselves from her forever.

One Saturday morning Mother called home from the library. "I've lost my bloomers," she said breathlessly.

"Oh, no," I cried out, and envisioned her walking down Main Street with her bloomers slipping down about her legs while everybody watched and snickered.

Eloise had heard my protest. "What is it, what's happened?" she asked, alarmed.

"Mother's lost her bloomers," I hissed.

"Where? Where did she lose them?" Eloise groaned.

"Where do you think you lost them?" I asked Mother, wishing Eloise had answered the telephone instead of me. "And couldn't you—couldn't you *feel* when they fell off?" Who had seen this terrible thing happen? Supposing Annabel or Margaret had seen Mother with her bloomers falling off downtown, or worse still, supposing *Chester* had seen it happen.

"Oh, not the pair I have on," and Mother sounded very casual, as though one lost bloomers every day. "My extra pair, the pair I was carrying with me in case the weather turns colder today. The paper said it might."

"It's her extra pair," I wailed to Eloise.

"I came straight down Fourth Street from home, and they were gone when I got to the library, so I'm sure they're somewhere on Fourth Street," Mother went on. "You'll see them, you can't miss them."

I would see them, I couldn't miss them! What in the world was she talking about? I wouldn't see them for anything in the world. If someone gave me a thousand dollars I would never lay claim to her bloomers lying someplace in a pink heap on Fourth Street.

"They're my good ones," Mother was saying. "Start out right now and pick them up and bring them on down to the library."

"I can't," I screamed. Surely she didn't know what she was asking. "I can't go get them."

But Mother was determined. "Hurry up, before someone picks them up."

"She wants you to find them for her," I told

Eloise when I had hung up the phone. "She said tell Eloise to bring them to me."

"*I* know what she said," Eloise replied, shuddering. "And you'd better get started."

There were only four blocks of Fourth Street to be traveled before reaching the library, but the blocks that I saw stretching ahead of me were endless ones, with a pair of pink bloomers in front of each house in each block, surrounded by a group of giggling people. Actually, however, there was no pair of bloomers in the first block, and I sighed with relief. Perhaps someone had already picked them up. Perhaps they were already safe in someone else's hands, someone who had no idea where they came from. Oh, that would be a wonderful thing; that would be good and kind of God.

Halfway down the second block I saw them, a pink heap in front of the Central Christian Church. I walked very slowly now. Just as I got to the church, a group of women came out.

"Look at this," one of them called out. "Look what somebody's lost."

"They're not mine," another woman called out gaily.

I walked with my head in the air. I saw no pink bloomers, I heard no words, no laughter. I was intent on something far down in the next block. I passed the bloomers by, turned to the right, and walked down Burkhart Street to Williams Street, and so on around the block and back to Fourth Street again at the beginning of the second block. There was no one on the block now but an old man on the other side of the street, and he would never know what I picked up. He was almost blind, you could tell by the way he tapped his stick along the sidewalk, and at that moment I loved him for his blindness.

Slowly, nonchalantly, carefully, I headed down the street.

"I'll lean over quickly," I thought. "I'll put them in my coat pocket, and walk on as though nothing had happened. Then in the next block I'll stuff them in good." This sounded like a good plan. This was not as bad as I had thought. I might be able to forgive Mother after all.

But the church was a fated spot. Almost as I reached the hideous pink lump in front of it, three men, one of them Mr. Hilton, came out of the church and walked toward me.

"Somebody's going to get cold," Mr. Hilton chuckled. Horrible man. The other two men looked down as he spoke and laughed heartily. "Women lose the darndest things," one of them said, and he gave the bloomers a kick that sent them sailing out into the street.

Mr. Hilton spoke to me jovially, but I merely said a quick hello, and pretended to be in a big hurry. This time I turned to the left, down Burkhart Street to Fifth Street, and back, until I again was at the beginning of the second block. I was exhausted by now. I had run almost all of the way and was gasping and panting so that I could scarcely breathe. I would not forgive Mother, either. I would not forgive Eloise; I was not even sure if I would forgive God. After letting Mother drop her bloomers in front of His own house, He had acted like this about my being able to pick them up. Sometimes God was a strange Being.

I knew this time there was no turning back. No matter who came along, even if Chester himself came out of the church, I had to get those bloomers. I could not survive another trip around the block. There was a black smudge on them where they had been kicked into the street; I could see this as I bent over to pick them up. That man had no right to kick them, they were Mother's good bloomers, they were her heavy silk ones that she wore to church and Eastern Star and to her clubs.

"Those won't fit you," someone called out in a loud hearty voice as I gathered up the bundle of revolting silk and started to stuff it into my pocket. It was Mr. Hilton, loud of voice and loud of laughter, coming out of the parsonage next to the church. He was alone, though; the other two men were not with him. When I turned around he looked funny, as though he wished he had not said anything. I tossed my head into the air. I had never actually retrieved a pair of smudged silk bloomers lying out in the street. I was Lady Gwendolyn Manners; I was walking down a wide marble stairway in a wonderful old English mansion. I was beautiful and proud and sure of myself. As Lady Gwendolyn I traversed the remaining blocks of Fourth Street and walked grandly and proudly into the library. But when I saw Mother and she asked expectantly, "Did you find them?" I began to sniffle. As far as I was concerned, everyone in Moberly had seen me picking up the bloomers; I was ruined forever, I was humiliated beyond all knowing.

"Those won't fit you, those won't fit you," I could hear Annabel and Margaret and Chester calling out, all sounding like Mr. Hilton.

Mother gave me fifteen cents for finding the bloomers, but all I wanted was to sink into the earth and never be seen again.

Mr. Hilton never mentioned the bloomer incident to me, but whenever I saw him after that and he smiled at me, I knew what he was smiling about. And even if he did not smile, I knew he was thinking about the bloomers. Probably he had told Mrs. Hilton, and it was not unlikely he had told all of the Boy Scouts. I was glad when the Hiltons moved away from Moberly. Mother said they were fine people, she was sorry to see them go. I never told her Mr. Hilton had seen me find her bloomers. Even at age twelve I had sense enough to know that it was not dignified for the town librarian to lose a pair of pink silk bloomers in front of the Central Christian Church.

16

THE ENCHANTED PRINCE

"No businessman is worth his salt," Mr. Carnegie believed, "who does not have his affairs so expertly organized that he can drop them at a moment's notice and leave for parts unknown." Naturally Mother had her affairs as well organized as Mr. Carnegie always had his; so, like Mr. Carnegie, she regularly took off, not for parts unknown — no respectable woman could do *that* — but for library conventions. This was an entertainment that Mr. Carnegie himself, with his love of libraries and his belief in the rounding out of a man's mind, would surely have approved of, would, in fact, have insisted upon. And being a man of propriety, he would doubtless also have approved of Mother's taking along her library chaperone.

I did not think it strange to be attending library conventions at a very early age, nor do I think this idea ever occurred to Mother. When she first started

264

going to the meetings, I was too young, she thought, to be left in the care of my older sisters. The American Library Association would give me more attention than *they* would, their young heads being filled only with thoughts of dates and dances and silliness. Besides, she hoped that I would learn something of value there.

Mother, who believed so strongly in exposing children to culture, thought that certainly some of the culture attached to masses of librarians would rub off on an impressionable child. I am not really sure about the culture rubbing off on me. My view of librarians, when I was between the ages of ten and twenty, was that they were all incredibly dull — not because they were librarians but because they were adults. And although I went dutifully to the conventions with Mother, it was not culture I was after, but the enchantment, the beautiful bluebird that one thinks can only be found out in the great world and never in one's own back yard.

I may as well admit that enchantment to me, from the time I read my first fairy tale, was synonymous with a knight in clanking armor or a prince from a far country. I did not demand that the object of my search wear a coat of silver metal or the ermine robe of a prince. I would recognize him, of course, even though he were disguised in a striped blazer and white flannels. But he never revealed himself to me in the vast auditoriums filled with book displays and library equipment and busy librarians.

Mother found in me a bookish individual some-what like herself. Our idea of a wonderful Saturday evening — at least before *I* discovered the joys of dates and dances and silliness — was a dime's worth of Woolworth candy and a new book from the library. Helen and Eloise, being older and more sophisticated, could take culture and Woolworth candy or leave them alone. I was a reasonably good traveling companion, since I was perfectly willing to curl up with a book on the train, and was not likely to embarrass or worry Mother by talking to strangers. Helen was especially bad about making friends with unknown persons when she was traveling, and Eloise, who was given to train sickness, was likely to announce "I'm going to throw up!" just as soon as the train had started.

Fortunately for Mother's peace of mind she did not know the inner me, did not know that the books and the library conventions which she thought were adding to my culture were also introducing me to the wonders and perils of life. Nor was she aware that I was much more dangerous than either of her other daughters because of the enchantment I constantly expected to find. Motion sickness and taking up with strangers on trains are annoying, but a seeker of enchantment is often wild and mad in a quiet, unrecognized manner until she has run off with the Sheik of Araby, or has been converted to a strange and unpopular religion, like one of Mother's great aunts, who joined the Sanctified

Holiness sect in her middle years and galloped up and down the country roads on her horse, shouting of the glory of the Lord. This, I secretly thought, remembering the joy Eloise and I had singing hymns on the way home from church, would have been wonderful fun. Thankfully, said Mother grimly, Aunt May did not live in town at this time, and had only the corn and the cows to hear her hallelujahs.

Neither Mother nor I was used to luxurious accommodations when we attended library conventions. If they were held in a town where we had family friends or relatives, obviously we stayed with them, sharing whatever our hosts had to offer. If this were not possible, we secured a room without bath at an inexpensive but genteel hotel, or sometimes even a rooming house — but always one recommended by the American Library Association — and I was advised to eat sparingly in restaurants. First of all, said Mother, who was a finicky eater, one could not trust restaurant food. Secondly, one was always likely to be exploited, especially at a time when a big convention was in town. We usually kept a sack of apples and a box of crackers in our hotel room for evening nibbling, and in my younger years I had a nickel to spend during the day for a chocolate phosphate or a candy bar, or any way I chose.

Cities surely must have been much safer in those days, because I remember wandering about by myself while Mother was in meetings, and although I was always to be at a certain spot at a certain hour, many of the dreadful dangers that now confront even adults in cities were not feared. The only thing I was frightened of – and this Mother had not mentioned, I had read of it in a book – was White Slavery. Mother had warned me early in life never to get into a car with a stranger, never to go off with anyone. (I would only have gone off with the sheik, an impoverished poet, the prince, or the knight.) When I was going through my White Slavery period, however, I was always wary, even when perfectly respectable male delegates to the conventions tried jovially to engage me in harmless conversation. Men in the White Slavery traffic, I knew, were often disguised as gentlemen, and even women would pretend to be kind and friendly until you were in their clutches. It was some comfort to read that one of the chief sources of supply of White Slaves was faraway England, where dissolute noblemen sent their prey to the Continent (my information on this was found in a book dating back to 1892) – but nevertheless, during this time I trusted very few persons. I was not at all sure what White Slavery really was, except that it left a mark of "vice unspeakable" on one's face – my freckles were bad enough; also, it was a state of "moral putrefaction" into which unhappy women creatures sank. Whatever it was, I sensed that it was not anything one discussed with one's mother. Women were ruined and could never go back home, that was for sure, and I had no wish to spend my life in hotels, even those recommended by the American Library Association.

I was in my eleventh summer when I disgraced Mother and myself at a national convention by screaming that I was being kidnapped, and accused a delegate from Minnesota of being a member of a White Slave ring. It all happened while I was waiting for Mother in a hotel lobby where she had said I must be at four o'clock sharp, when she was supposed to emerge from a meeting in one of the halls of the same hotel. She did not come at four, and she was still not in sight by four-thirty, and I had grown tired of pretending I was a debutante waiting to be taken to a dinner dance by a millionaire—and also a little bit frightened. Mother was seldom late. A gentleman sitting on the other side of the potted palm kept staring at me, and this made me even more nervous. He was doubtless a White Slaver— even though he was well dressed and looked respectable—and he knew I was alone, but I did not dare leave my post. This was only the first day of the convention, and our hotel was in a residential area a long streetcar ride away.

"Little girl," the man finally said, coming over to me solicitously, "are you lost?"

I was too frightened to answer him.

"Are you staying in this hotel?"

But I still refused to speak, only staring at him

wildly.

"Well, let's go over to the desk and see if we can find out where you belong," he said heartily, and took me by the arm.

It was then I screamed, because a White Slaver, I knew, would simply walk off with a child and say it was his own. Many a little girl had ended up in Brussels or Paris from just such a chance episode.

And it was then that Mother, much too late, reached her appointed spot at the potted palm.

"What's going on here?" she asked, terrified.

"I was only trying to help this little girl," the man said confusedly. "She looked as though she was lost."

A crowd had gathered, and the desk attendant himself had pushed his way hastily through the group, and asked the man angrily what he was trying to do.

"I happen to be a librarian from Minneapolis," the man said haughtily, "here attending the ALA convention. And *this* is what one gets for trying to be a good Samaritan."

It was then he called me a nasty little girl, and, noticing Mother's ALA identification badge on her dress, told her she was a disgrace to her profession, teaching me about such things as White Slavery. Mother, outraged, asked where *his* badge was; for all she knew I was right, and it was a good thing I had sense enough to scream when I was touched by a stranger, for child-molesters were not unknown, even in libraries.

"Where in the name of heaven did you ever hear about White Slavery?" she asked me curiously as we were riding to our own hotel.

"Why, in the library," I answered, surprised. Where else would I find books to read? "Back in the W's someplace, I think. Or in the Y's. A Salvation Army history."

Washington, Seattle, Atlantic City – these names roll gloriously on my tongue as though I were calling the list of towns in the big-time vaudeville circuit. Mother and I attended meetings of the ALA in all of these places and many more between 1920 and 1936.

I do not remember all the names of Mother's friends at the conventions, but occasionally, going through the family album, I see them smiling from the official pictures, or come across photographs sent to her in their Christmas letters. Mother was an outgoing person and had many friends in her home town, but just as many, I think, that she had made on her trips to the ALA conventions. Many of them were younger than she, since she had started her library career in her middle age, plunged by widowhood from the haven of protected housewife, mother, and clubwoman into the world of "the public" – a violent but certain cure for sorrow.

Mother carried on fairly constant correspondence with many of the lady librarians she met at the meetings. They would greet each other yearly with cries of delight, and plan extracurricular activities that the convention planners might have over-looked, such as tours of the city and visits to historic monuments. Part of the pleasure of the conventions for Mother was planning for them during the entire year, and learning in advance everything about the cities in which they were being held. She believed in getting her money's worth on a trip, and was determined to see all the sights in every town she visited.

"Look," she would point out to me on our travels, "you may never have a chance to see this again." It was as though the marvel, be it monument, river, or museum, could endure only if protected in our memories.

It is true Mother could not bring herself to take a sight-seeing trip by airplane over Washington, D.C., but she sent me as her emissary, suffering anguish, I am sure, at the danger to which she was exposing me, but believing the benefit to me from such an experience to outweigh the risks. Accompanying me on this wild, dangerous flight, which soared so close to the Washington Monument that I was almost able to touch it, was one of her younger and braver friends, Miss Nellie Dewey, No Kin to Mr. You-Know-Who-ey. This is how Miss Nellie Dewey liked to introduce herself, and it always caused a roar of appreciative laughter. To this day I meet intelligent, well-read individuals who think that it was John Dewey — or maybe even Tom! — who was responsible for the Dewey library cataloguing system. *I* knew about Melvil and his work at an early age.

I also knew the importance of the date 1876. While other children thought they were smart remembering 1776, to me 1876 held fully as much meaning. Mother and Miss Nellie Dewey and her friends often bemoaned the fact that they could not have attended the first library convention held in Philadelphia in that momentous year — even Mother had not been born in time for that great event. Mother, who was something of a library historian, was familiar with the public library movement in the United States, and felt on extremely familiar terms with Dewey, Justin Winsor, William Frederick Poole, Charles Ammi Cutter, and all the rest of the gentlemen active in the second half of the nineteenth century. She was most interested in the early conferences she read about and the entertainment provided to the librarians then, but was not at all impressed by the fact that librarians attending a conference in Milwaukee in 1886 were given a trip to a brewery and shown the processes used in making beer. They actually sampled "the product of the establishment." She did not like to think that back in Moberly the taxpayers might think *she* was going to beer parties when she went off to library conventions. She and Miss Nellie Dewey and some of her other friends discussed all this at great length as being harmful to the image of the librarians. It made them look, said Miss Nellie, like carnival roisterers. Then she and Mother giggled, grown-up, appalling giggles that embarrassed me.

Unlike me, Mother was not looking for enchantment at the library conventions. She had had it and had lost it when my father died. Library conventions were serious business with her. They were part of her work; they enlarged her intellectual and professional world; in a sense they provided postgraduate courses to keep her on her toes. And perhaps it was because Mother was not searching for enchantment—for such is the way of life—that she found it at one of the library conventions, even though she chose to pass it by.

Sometimes I look carefully over the photographs in our family album to see if I can find Mother's Library Beau. Strangely enough, however, I realize that I would not really know him if he was there. For it was so long ago—and was it at a state or a national convention that she met him? All I can truly remember is that I thought he was old, as I thought anyone over twenty was old, and my voice, my hideous, youthful voice, rings down the years telling her so and giggling. He was possibly only her own age, perhaps slightly older; even, for all I know, younger.

Mother was not a femme fatale, although in her youth she had been extremely pretty. Naturally, as her daughter, I thought her rather dowdy and her ideas completely antiquated. Her only cosmetic when I was young was prepared chalk applied with a chamois skin, but she indulged in one dreadful practice that my sisters and I found humiliating and unmotherly. She dyed her hair. Other mothers in those days grayed as mothers should, but my mother's bobbed hair got blacker and blacker with the years. When my grandmother taxed her about this, Mother replied determinedly that this deception was necessary when one worked with the public.

It was not until years later that my sisters and I were able to understand that the library was Mother's salvation. Her position as librarian gave her what we, with our youthful arrogance, could not, a sense of importance, of her own worth. It filled her days and her nights, for those were the years when librarians worked long hours that would make today's professionals scream for the unions. The library conventions were the main events in her life.

The first I remember of Mother's Library Beau at one of the meetings is that he took Mother and me to a circus. I am rather sure the circus was not a part of the ALA program and that he must have done this as a special favor to me. Fortunately for Mother's Library Beau, as well as for all the male delegates, by this summer I had emerged from my fear of White Slavery. Mature and sophisticated, I was going through my Sara Teasdale period, and was expecting momentarily to meet a lover named Colin or Robin or Strephon. I wanted nothing more than to be haunted night and day, as Sara Teasdale was, by the kiss in Colin's eyes. Nevertheless, I was not too grown-up for circuses.

One event of the day stands out in my memory. A zebra running in parade around the circus track with other animals escaped briefly from his fellows and ran toward the section in which we were seated, and Mother, who had brought an umbrella, picked it up and brandished it like a sword at the approaching animal.

"How brave you were, Carrie!" her Beau told her admiringly after the zebra had been corralled and the audience had settled down. He, too, had been brave, and had leaped gallantly from his seat to battle, if need be, the frantic zebra. I had found Mother's actions embarrassing and hoped no one knew she was my mother. In later years I was able to realize that Mother must have spent a great deal of her widowed life courageously brandishing umbrellas at onrushing zebras — putting three daughters through college; maintaining a home for us in the days when a coal furnace had to be kept going, ashes taken out, a garden kept, snow shoveled; as well as doing a man's job of providing a living; and pathetically fighting the terrors of an old age when she could not work, with her little bottle of black hair dye.

At the end of the circus day, after I had been sated with entertainment, cotton candy, and pink lemonade, and Mother and I were alone in our hotel room, Mother asked me, rather shyly for her, how I liked her friend. That was when I muttered, without interest or any intention of cruelty, how old he was, and snickered.

I remarked mischievously about Mother's Library Beau when we returned home, telling about Mother and me being taken to dinner and movies and on special tours by him, and my sisters questioned me curiously. Also, I believe, a few letters came, because I remember one of my sisters saying wisely as she picked up an envelope that had just come in the mail, "It's from *him*."

Whatever her personal feelings at that time, Mother kept her thoughts to herself. Before we had left the convention meeting, Miss Nellie Dewey and Miss Allen had teased her a little, and one or two others of her friends had asked her archly, "What's this I hear?" or "I understand that Peggy has a handsome admirer." But Mother did not encourage their curiosity.

Certainly I never saw Mother's Library Beau again. Whether or not she did, I have no idea. Since nothing more came of it, I am hopeful that she had no more wish to marry him than she had one or two other beaux who had courted her after my father's death. She had, after all, her books. And three lively daughters. And she was not really a woman alone in the world, as the library patrons and even her friends believed her to be. Sometimes at home, when she was working out in the garden and thought no one could hear, I had heard her whisper my father's name, "Oh, Luther, Luther," as though he were right beside her. And when she was down in the library, of course, she had Mr. Carnegie to guard her.

There was one change in our lives, however. Mother no longer went yearly to the library conventions. Sometimes one or two years would go by without a trip to the meetings. Our last was in 1935, in Denver. I had just graduated from college and could not have cared less about a library convention. All I wanted was to return home to see the boy to whom I had become engaged. For I had found enchantment at last at journalism school in college. The knight was not wearing a suit of armor but a battered felt hat pushed back off his forehead in the fashion of aspiring journalists of that period. I remember Mother asking me if I thought I would ever like to be a librarian, in case I did not get a job on a newspaper, which was my dream. I responded dramatically that I would rather die than be anything but a reporter. Fortunately I achieved this ambition shortly thereafter at a salary of ten dollars a week. Even librarians, I am sure, were doing better than that, but then they did not have by-lines.

Years later, after my mother's death, I came across a letter from one of her librarian friends with whom she had corresponded for years and who had married rather late. They always addressed each other formally, Miss Allen, Mrs. Elsea.

"I wish you could meet Bert," Miss Allen, by then Mrs. Brooks, had written to my mother. "I have known such happiness with him, even though this has come so late in our lives. You will be interested to know that he looks somewhat like your David, tall, imposing, very handsome (I think), and a very gentle nature."

At first I could not conceive who the David of Miss Allen's letter could be. My father's name was Luther, and David was a name alien to my acquaintance. Off to the side of the sentence, however, in Mother's handwriting, I saw lightly penciled and underlined the words, "My David," just as she had underlined the words *tall, imposing, very handsome, and a very gentle nature.* I realized then with a shock that David must have been the name of Mother's Library Beau. I had thought so little of him that I had never even asked his first name.

In the last few years I have leafed more and more often through the family album. There is a section devoted entirely to Mother as librarian — Mother winning fourth prize in 1932 in a Librarians' Buying Information Contest sponsored by the H. W. Wilson Company; Mother in 1927 participating in a round-table discussion of library index systems at the annual meeting of the Missouri Library Association; Mother visiting the grave of the benefactor of the Moberly library — Andrew Carnegie — in Tarrytown, New York, on the ninth anniversary of his death, a sentimental journey that I feel would have pleased him enormously.

From time to time I stop before a picture of a group of librarians and wonder if any of the men I am staring at is the Enchanted Prince of Mother's middle age. Does one of these black and white ghosts wear a suit of armor invisible to my eyes? Does an unseen ermine cloak fall regally from the shoulders of one of the sedate, dignified gentlemen gazing back at me from the twenties? Someplace, in an attic, in an old album, scribbled on the side of a letter written by my mother, perhaps, or under an ALA photograph in which Mother appears, is there another notation that I shall never see? — the nostalgic, wistful words, "My Carrie."

DATE DUE
